PENGUIN PASSNOTES

As You Like It

Dr Stephen Coote was educated at Cambridge and at London University. He was Director of Studies and Head of English at tutorial colleges in London and Oxford. He has written a number of other guides in the Passnotes series, including *Wuthering Heights, Twelfth Night, Macbeth* and *Chaucer: The Prologue to the Canterbury Tales.*

PENGUIN PASSNOTES

WILLIAM SHAKESPEARE

As You Like It

STEPHEN COOTE, M.A., PH.D.

PENGUIN BOOKS

Penguin Books Ltd, Harmondsworth, Middlesex, England
Viking Penguin Inc., 40 West 23rd Street, New York, New York 10010,U.S.A.
Penguin Books Australia Ltd, Ringwood, Victoria, Australia
Penguin Books Canada Limited, 2801 John Street, Markham, Ontario, Canada L3R 1B4
Penguin Books (N.Z.) Ltd, 182–190 Wairau Road, Auckland 10, New Zealand

First published 1985
Reprinted 1986

Made and printed in Great Britain by
Richard Clay (The Chaucer Press) Ltd, Bungay, Suffolk
Filmset in 10/12pt Monophoto Ehrhardt by
Northumberland Press Ltd, Gateshead, Tyne and Wear

*The publishers are grateful to the following Examination Boards for
permission to reproduce questions from examination papers used in
individual titles in the Passnotes series:*

*Associated Examining Board, University of Cambridge Local Examinations
Syndicate, Joint Matriculation Board, University of London School
Examinations Department, Oxford and Cambridge Schools Examination
Board, University of Oxford Delegacy of Local Examinations.*

*The Examination Boards accept no responsibility whatsoever for the accuracy or
method of working in any suggested answers given as models.*

Contents

To the Student

This book is designed to help you with your O-level or C.S.E. English Literature examinations. It contains an introduction to the play, analysis of scenes and characters, and a commentary on some of the issues raised by the text. Line references are to the New Penguin Shakespeare, edited by H. J. Oliver.

When you use this book, remember that it is no more than an aid to your study. It will help you to find passages quickly and perhaps give you some ideas for essays. But remember: *This book is not a substitute for reading the play, and it is your response and your knowledge that matter*. These are the things that the examiners are looking for, and they are also the things that will give you the most pleasure. Show your knowledge and appreciation to the examiner, and show them clearly.

Introduction:
Background to As You Like It

As You Like It takes us into a comic world of disguised princesses, cruel tyrants, marvellous adventures and surprise happy endings. At its heart lies the dream of pastoral happiness, of life in the forests and fields, where love is the chief occupation. To appreciate the play we must enjoy its artificiality, its world of make-believe. We must also learn to see its variety of moods, its moments of sudden seriousness, rapture and satire.

Shakespeare combines these elements through a rich variety of characters. We are shown Rosalind, clever, brave and loving. She is a woman who throws herself into whatever life offers, who watches and participates and eventually helps to bring about the happy ending. We meet Celia, her close friend. Then there is Orlando, the young, vigorous man battling with an unhappy fate and eventually falling hopelessly in love, who emerges at the end married and secure. Touchstone, the court jester, amuses us through his wit and word-play. The rustics – Corin, Silvius, William, Audrey and Phebe – delight us, while Jaques keeps us constantly aware of the touch of foolishness in all people – even himself. Finally, we move through a world of good rulers who have been deposed and of evil men like Oliver and Duke Frederick who undergo sudden conversions.

The play presents a wide range of themes. We see something of the variety of love: trusting friendship, compassion, loyalty, the rapturous discovery of boy meeting girl. Sometimes the lovers are cruel, at other times they are foolish. Over them all presides Rosalind with her natural spirits and high intelligence. We also learn how melancholy follows lovers and how disguise conceals their real natures from each other. Finally, we see how all true love is concluded in marriage.

As You Like It is a delightful work that stretches our imaginations and provides a great deal of pleasure. But it is not an easy play. Just as much of the action and many of the characters are highly artificial, so much of the language is complex, punning and not always easy to understand. To be fully appreciated, the play needs to be studied carefully, using the notes in our copy of the text so that we are sure we really understand what is being said. When we are confident that we can follow the meaning, then we can see *As You Like It* as a play that provides an endless source of pleasure and entertainment.

Synopsis

Orlando, the youngest son of Sir Rowland de Boys, is cruelly treated by his eldest brother, Oliver. He has been denied money, education and respect. He opens the play by complaining of his misfortunes to Adam, an old family retainer. When Oliver enters, a quarrel breaks out between the two brothers. Orlando upbraids Oliver for the treatment he has received and demands that he be either given his rights or offered the small inheritance left him by his father. He then departs.

When Orlando has left, Oliver's evil nature becomes yet clearer. He summons Charles, the royal wrestler, and we learn that this man is to play a part in Oliver's plans to rid himself of Orlando for ever. During their ensuing conversation we also learn a number of other important facts. First, there has been a revolt in the country. The old Duke (called throughout the play 'Duke Senior') has been dethroned and exiled by his younger brother, Frederick. Duke Senior is now living in the Forest of Arden. He and the gentlemen who flock to him there live a delightful life. Secondly, we hear of Rosalind, Duke Senior's daughter. She has not followed her father into exile but is living in the court with her great friend and cousin, Celia, the daughter of the usurping Duke. The two girls are inseparable. Oliver then raises the subject of the forthcoming wrestling match. The wrestler, Charles, tells how he has heard that Orlando is determined to come and try his strength against him. He asks Oliver to dissuade him from this because he does not wish to hurt Orlando, which, he believes, he must do if the young man does indeed come to the fight. Oliver begins to blacken his brother's reputation. He tells Charles that Orlando is an evil, deceitful young man who will, in all probability, try and find some way of doing harm to Charles. The wrestler is both amazed and convinced by this. He swears that he will now defeat Orlando with pleasure. Oliver, left on his own, hopes that he has seen the end of Orlando. Nonetheless, he cannot explain the fanatical hatred he has for the young man. He recognizes that his brother is virtuous and a gentleman, despite his lack of education. Oliver resents the love that all the people seem to have for him and is happy that he has at last found a way to have Orlando removed. He leaves to make sure that Orlando will indeed attend the wrestling match.

The second scene introduces us to Rosalind and Celia. Celia is trying to comfort her cousin, who is sorrowing for her banished father. She points out their depth of friendship and emphasizes her loyalty to her friend. She begs her to be more cheerful. With the natural liveliness that makes Rosalind such an attractive character, she suddenly suggests they divert themselves by falling in love. And it is about love, women and fortune that they are talking when Touchstone, the court jester, enters. He bids Celia come before her father. The two girls jest with him, and Touchstone's answers reveal his quick wit and ready affection. As the three characters joke, Le Beau, a ridiculous courtier, enters. He has been ordered to bring Celia to the wrestling match, but Rosalind, Celia and Touchstone derive much amusement at his expense before he can describe the wrestling to them. He finally tells them a sad story of how an old father lost three of his sons as Charles broke their bones in the wrestling ring. Touchstone declares that this is barely suitable entertainment for ladies.

The court enters. Duke Frederick has been trying to dissuade Orlando from fighting, but to no avail. Rosalind and Celia ask to meet him. Celia requests him not to fight, and Rosalind supports her. Orlando asks to be allowed to take part and begs the girls to wish him well. After all, he says, he has nothing to live for, and, if he dies, it will be no real loss. Rosalind, who has started to fall in love, wishes on Orlando the 'little strength' she has. The fight then begins, the Duke having declared that it will end after the first fall. As the fight progresses, so it becomes clear that Orlando is the more able wrestler. Eventually he throws Charles, who is carried off. Duke Frederick comes across to congratulate Orlando, who tells him his name and birth. The Duke is grieved to hear these. Sir Rowland de Boys, Orlando's father, was a close friend of the Duke whose throne Frederick has usurped. Orlando's very presence reminds Frederick of his treachery.

Orlando is left alone with Rosalind and Celia. Rosalind's love becomes clearer. She offers Orlando a golden chain and, as they leave, longs to return to the young man. She can only call out farewell.

Orlando has fallen deeply and suddenly in love with Rosalind. He is left wondering at his emotions as Le Beau returns to tell him that Duke Frederick is a man of quickly changing moods. He is now violently opposed to Orlando. Orlando thanks Le Beau for the information and then asks whether either of the two girls he has just met is Duke Frederick's daughter. Le Beau somewhat laboriously explains that Celia is the Duke's daughter, while Rosalind is the daughter of the exiled Duke Senior. Rosalind too, he says, has become an enemy of Duke Frederick's. She is too popular, too much loved. The Duke's malice against her will no doubt suddenly break out.

Orlando, left alone, shows how he is caught between the hatred of the Duke and the hatred of his brother. He also makes clear his burgeoning love for Rosalind.

The third scene reintroduces us to Rosalind and Celia. Again, Rosalind is unhappy. This time it is because she is in love. The two girls begin to discuss Orlando as Duke Frederick enters and, as Le Beau had predicted, he turns his anger on Rosalind and banishes her from the court. She is given ten days in which to flee. She eloquently pleads her own defence, but Duke Frederick is firm in his tyranny. Celia tries to plead for her cousin and forcibly urges Rosalind's innocence. The Duke calls his daughter a fool. Can she not see that the great affection Rosalind arouses robs Celia of her due? Celia retorts that if Rosalind is banished, then so is she. The Duke leaves, once again confirming his order of exile.

Celia tries to comfort Rosalind. She declares that she will go into exile with her. She proposes that they seek out Rosalind's father in the Forest of Arden and adds that to avoid danger they should dress themselves poorly and dirty their faces. Rosalind's spirits rise. She suggests that to further the disguise she should dress herself up as a man and call herself Ganymede. Celia declares that she will call herself Aliena. Finally, Rosalind suggests they take Touchstone along with them. They leave to collect their jewels and lay their plans.

Act II opens with Duke Senior in the Forest of Arden. He praises the life that he and his co-exiles lead, and one of the Lords mentions 'the melancholy Jaques', a man who delights in satirizing the weaknesses of his fellow men. The courtier offers an amusing description of Jaques moralizing on the death of a deer and thoroughly enjoying his bitter thoughts. The Duke is delighted by this, and the Lords offer to take him to where Jaques may be found.

Act II, Scene ii, is brief and harsh. The usurping Duke Frederick has discovered that Rosalind and Celia have fled the court, apparently without being seen by anyone. An attendant Lord then tells how Touchstone the clown is also missing. He adds that the court gossip has it that Celia and Rosalind have been much taken by Orlando. Hisperia, Celia's maid, is reported to be sure that wherever the girls have gone, Orlando is bound to be in their company. The furious Duke commands Oliver to be brought before him. He will be ordered to seek out his brother. The Duke leaves, demanding that 'these foolish runaways' be hunted down with the utmost vigilance.

In fact, Orlando has not met up with Rosalind, Celia and Touchstone. He has returned home after his victory at the wrestling match. He is met by Adam in a great state of perturbation. Orlando tries to calm the old man down, and eventually learns from him that Oliver intends to burn Orlando in his bed or, if that fails, to find some other way of killing him. Adam urges Orlando to flee at all costs. But where, he asks, can he go? Besides, he has no money and so will be forced either to beg or to become a thief. His natural sense of honour forbids him either course, and he concludes that it would be better for him to stay at home. What follows is deeply touching. Old Adam offers Orlando his lifetime's savings, the money he has put by against the time he should be an example of 'unregarded age in corners thrown'. He also begs to be allowed to go with Orlando on his journey. The young man is moved. He warns Adam that he is unable to pay back the loan, but accepts both the old man's offer and his company. Together, they go off to seek their fortunes.

The fourth scene reintroduces us to Rosalind, Celia and Touchstone. The two girls had set off for the Forest of Arden in high spirits. Now they have arrived, but are exhausted to the point of tears. Touchstone thinks he would have been better off at home. The pastoral world, it seems, is not all a delightful idyll. Nonetheless, it has its amusing side. As the three travellers lament their plight, a pair of shepherds appear. Silvius, the younger of the two, is deeply – even hopelessly – in love. His fine poetic language and refined emotions form an amusing contrast to his local accent and working man's clothes. Here, we may say, is the standard lovelorn shepherd of the pastoral convention (see pp. 33, 84–7). But Silvius is presented in such a way that we smile at him. Like all true lovers, Silvius has been drawn into 'many actions most ridiculous'. Suddenly he breaks away from Corin, his elderly companion, and runs off sighing after his beloved Phebe.

His lover's pangs remind Rosalind of her own feelings for Orlando. Touchstone too is reminded of an affair of his youth. Celia, who has not yet fallen in love, somewhat more practically suggests that Touchstone go and ask the older shepherd for food. The clown obeys. Touchstone thinks of himself as the sophisticated man of the court surrounded by country yokels. He addresses Corin in an amusingly absurd and condescending manner. Rosalind is embarrassed by this and asks Corin in a more direct and polite way for rest and food. Remember that at this point Rosalind is disguised as the boy Ganymede, and so it is appropriate for her to ask protection for the weary Aliena. While we may be amused by Corin's apparent simplicity, we should also be touched by his natural kindness and dignity. He confesses that the life he lives is a harsh one, that his master is cruel and that the farm on which he works is about to be sold. Nonetheless, he bids all three of them welcome. Rosalind is then told that the farm is about to be sold to none other than the young Silvius, though, in his present state, the lover 'little cares for buying anything'. This is the quick-witted Rosalind's opportunity. She suggests that they buy the farm themselves and have Corin manage it for them. (They have, you will remember, brought their jewels with them to provide for just such emergencies.) Celia agrees. The pastoral life is attractive to her too. Corin is delighted by his change of fortune and willingly agrees to be their employee.

Act II, Scene v opens with a song performed by Lord Amiens, one of the courtiers to Duke Senior. When the song is over, Jaques, who has been listening, begs for more. A witty exchange follows between the courtiers and Jaques, who confesses that he 'can suck melancholy out of a song, as a weasel sucks eggs'. Eventually the courtiers sing another stanza and, when this is over, Jaques makes up a satirical third verse. Having called the courtiers fools, he leaves them.

Old Adam is exhausted by the long journey to the Forest of Arden. At the beginning of Act II, Scene vi, he is fainting with hunger and fatigue. Orlando spurs him on and vows to provide for him. For a moment he thinks of leaving the old man while he goes off to look for food, but then realizes that he must not leave him on his own. He carries him off to find protection.

Duke Senior has been searching for Jaques but has not found him. Jaques then enters, but, far from being his usual melancholy self, he is actually laughing. He tells us why. He has met Touchstone in the forest, and the clown's mixture of foolish words and wisdom appeals deeply to Jaques. He too would like to be a professional fool. Such a role in life would give him the opportunity to say what he pleased about people: to laugh at them and satirize them. He promises that such behaviour would only do good. Interestingly, the Duke points out that for all his railing on vice, Jaques himself has been a 'libertine', a loose-living man. The vices which he attacks he has himself committed. Jaques denies that he satirizes anyone in particular. Only those who are actually guilty of what he attacks will feel the sting in what he says.

The debate is violently interrupted by Orlando. With sword drawn he orders the royal party to stop eating, even though, as Jaques points out, they have not yet started their meal. To the Duke, it is evident that Orlando is a man of some breeding, and he politely asks him if he is in distress. Orlando replies that he is and again demands food. The Duke bids him join them. Orlando is abashed by his courtesy. He recognizes that the Duke must have seen better days too, and then explains that he must fetch old Adam. While he does so, Jaques delivers the famous 'Seven Ages of Man' speech, a bitter account of man's weakness and decline towards death. As Jaques finishes, so Orlando enters bearing the exhausted Adam. Active charity and kindness are strongly contrasted to Jaques' cynicism. The party sits down to eat. Amiens diverts them with another song. Orlando tells his story to the Duke, who, pleased to meet the son of his old friend Sir Rowland de Boys, invites him to stay in his cave.

Act III is mainly concerned with love in the pastoral world, but it opens with a short and violent scene in the usurper's court. Duke Frederick has summoned Oliver before him. He orders him to seek out Orlando. If he does not find him 'within this twelvemonth', he will be banished. In the meantime, the Duke seizes Oliver's possessions.

Safe in the pastoral world, Orlando can indulge his love for Rosalind. He runs around the forest and, like Silvius, is drawn into 'many actions most ridiculous'. These include pinning his rather poor love-poems to the trees. Corin and Touchstone are left to discuss the pastoral life.

Corin's directness and simplicity are again both amusing and rather touching. Touchstone's wit meanwhile allows us to see the contrast between a highly intelligent man of the court and a simple shepherd. Touchstone amusingly proves that Corin's innocent life actually leads to damnation.

Rosalind enters reading one of Orlando's verses. Touchstone immediately offers a parody of it. Celia then enters reading another of the young man's poems. The two women ask to be left alone. They joke about the quality of Orlando's poetry. Celia then makes Rosalind recognize that the poet is none other than her beloved Orlando. The intense excitement of Rosalind's young love becomes immediately apparent. Celia teases her gently, but Rosalind's spirits – despite her disguise as a man – are irrepressible. Orlando then passes by. He is engaging in mildly comic abuse with the melancholy Jaques. When the older man has left, Rosalind determines to speak to the lovelorn Orlando 'like a saucy lackey'. A witty exchange follows. Orlando becomes interested in the 'boy' who talks to him in such an amusing way. Orlando confesses that he is in love, and Rosalind – still disguised as Ganymede – offers to cure him of his affliction. But, she adds, Orlando has none of the usual marks of a true lover. Orlando protests that his passion is sincere. Rosalind again offers to cure it. She tells Orlando that he is to take her (in her disguise as Ganymede) for his true love. She will then prove so contrary, so difficult, that, like another she has cured, he will eventually lose all desire to love and lead a monastic life. The unsuspecting Orlando is finally won over to her plan.

There are other lovers in the Forest of Arden. Touchstone has fallen in with a country wench called Audrey, and as they talk and Touchstone exercises his wit on the simple girl, they are watched by Jaques. Eventually, Touchstone proposes marriage. The vicar, it would appear, is already lined up. When he arrives, there is no one to give Audrey away. Jaques steps forward, but manages to persuade Touchstone out of being 'married under a bush like a beggar'. The vicar, Sir Oliver Martext, is considerably put out.

Orlando has failed to turn up on time for his meeting with Rosalind, who, of course, is still disguised as Ganymede. She is concerned and bitter. Celia believes that Orlando is not really in love at all. Rosalind describes how, when she met her father in the forest, he did not recognize her because of her disguise. However, Orlando is more important to her than her father. Corin enters to tell them that Silvius and Phebe are near at hand. Rosalind and Celia go off to watch these pastoral lovers.

Act III, Scene v, is delightfully comic. Silvius, the shepherd boy, is still hopelessly in love. Phebe is playing the cruel-hearted lady, a role which, as Rosalind will make clear, ill becomes her. Phebe quickly destroys all Silvius's poetic fancies with her cold common sense. She then decides to cause Silvius a great deal more suffering. Rosalind chooses to intervene at this point. Still disguised as Ganymede, she steps forward and roundly chides Phebe for her hard-heartedness. Phebe is immediately entranced by this seeming youth's harsh tones and falls deeply in love. Rosalind leaves, having told Phebe to be less disdainful towards Silvius. But Phebe is now hopelessly in love with Rosalind disguised as Ganymede, and begins to see that Silvius may have his uses after all. When she has very touchingly described her feelings, Phebe vows to write to Ganymede a stern letter. Silvius will deliver it.

Act IV opens with an encounter between Rosalind and Jaques. Jaques tries to impress, while Rosalind shows herself to be witty and resilient. When Orlando eventually appears, she chides him for his lateness. In the exchange that follows he protests his undying love, while Rosalind questions his feelings. Her own become apparent. Rosalind is here both witty and deeply serious. Orlando realizes that he has an appointment to attend the Duke at dinner. Rosalind begs him not to break his promise to come on time again and he departs. Celia, meanwhile, is horrified by how forward Rosalind has been. 'You have simply misused our sex', she says. But Rosalind is so deeply in love – and expresses this so movingly – that such proprieties no longer matter to her.

The second scene of Act IV is a brief interlude in which the hunters sing a song. The scene acts as a break between the love we have just witnessed and the arrival of Silvius with Phebe's letter.

Yet again – and despite his promise – Orlando is late. We shall learn the reason for this in a moment or two. In the meantime, Silvius arrives with Phebe's letter. Rosalind reads it and is amazed by its forthright tones. At first she thinks that Silvius must have written it. He denies this and, when he hears its contents, is enraptured by the mere sound of Phebe's words. Rosalind calls him a fool for loving such a woman and tells him to return to Phebe and say that if she does love Ganymede, then Ganymede bids her to love Silvius. As he departs, Oliver enters. He, of course, has been sent out by Duke Frederick to find Orlando. However, he has a different story to tell. It emerges that he has come to the girls at Orlando's bidding to find the boy Orlando calls his Rosalind. When Oliver has established that he has indeed found the person he is looking for, he reveals that he has been further charged to present Rosalind with 'this bloody napkin'.

At Rosalind's eager request, Oliver tells his story. Orlando, Oliver says, left Rosalind a while ago in order to attend the Duke at dinner. As he was wandering through the forest and meditating on love, he saw a wretched man asleep on his back with a snake coiled round his neck. Seeing Orlando, the snake slid away watched by a lioness that was hiding in the undergrowth and waiting to pounce. Orlando approached the sleeping man and saw that he was none other than his own treacherous brother. (At this point in the story none of the listeners on stage know that the teller of this tale is in fact Oliver himself.) At first, Orlando wanted to leave Oliver there to be ravaged by the lioness. It seemed only fair revenge. Twice he turned from him. However, his good nature eventually won him over and he turned back and slew the lioness. The noise of the fight woke Oliver, who now reveals his true name to his listeners.

Both Rosalind and Celia know of Oliver's past wickedness, but, Oliver declares, he is now a reformed character. Oliver goes on to tell how Orlando took him to the Duke's cave and, when Oliver had been given new clothes in exchange for his rags, how Orlando showed him the wounds he had received in the fight with the lioness. These wounds caused Orlando to faint. As he did so, he cried out for his Rosalind. Oliver bound up his wounds and, when he had revived, Orlando bade him take the 'bloody napkin' to Rosalind and explain the reason for his failure to attend their promised meeting. Rosalind, betraying her true nature under her boy's disguise, faints. When she revives, she claims that she was only pretending. Oliver is not convinced. However, he helps Celia to carry Rosalind to their cottage.

Act V opens with Touchstone and Audrey. She is impatient at not being married. Touchstone, however, realizes that he may have a rival for her love. This rival – a country boy named William – now enters. Touchstone is again given the opportunity to show off his wit. In long, comically pompous sentences, he tells William to leave Audrey alone or fight a duel. William, who is capable of few words of more than one syllable, leaves. When he has gone, Corin enters to summon Touchstone before Celia.

Oliver too has fallen in love. Orlando asks him if he can really have taken to Celia so quickly. He has indeed, and she is in love with him. Oliver vows that they will live out a pastoral life together and offers Orlando the whole of his estates. Orlando agrees to their marriage as Rosalind enters. Again, he confesses his love for Rosalind. She, still disguised as Ganymede, describes how deeply Celia has fallen in love with Oliver. Orlando declares that they are to be married tomorrow and then thinks of his own wretchedly lonely state. Ganymede will no longer serve for him, and Rosalind realizes that she must plan a way to reveal her true self. She claims she has magic powers learned from an uncle and will use these to bring the real Rosalind before Orlando when his brother marries Celia. Orlando can barely believe her, but she promises to be as good as her word. Silvius and Phebe then enter. Phebe blames Rosalind – whom she still believes to be the boy Ganymede – for revealing to Silvius the contents of her letter. In an amusing passage, the lovers all confess their emotions and Rosalind silences them by promising to settle their affairs the following day. With that, she leaves.

The third scene of Act V is a delightful musical interlude in which two of the Duke's pages sing for Touchstone and Audrey after the clown has declared he will marry his wench the following day.

The last scene of the play brings all the various plots to their resolution. The Duke asks Orlando if he believes Ganymede can really do all that was promised. Orlando is caught between hope and doubt. Rosalind, still disguised as Ganymede, enters. She makes all the characters repeat their promises. The Duke promises he will offer Rosalind, when she appears, to Orlando. Orlando promises to accept her. Phebe promises to marry Ganymede if he is willing and, if Phebe refuses him, to wed Silvius. Silvius promises to marry Phebe if such an unlikely event should ever occur. With the promise to fulfil all of this repeated, Rosalind leaves. As she goes, Rosalind's manner reminds the Duke of his daughter (who, of course, she is) and Orlando agrees about the likeness, though he swears that Ganymede has been born and bred in the forest. Touchstone and Audrey now enter, much to Jaques's delight. Touchstone proceeds to amuse the courtiers with a satire on duelling, lying and courtly behaviour. When he has finished, a 'masquer', or actor, dressed as Hymen, the God of Marriage, enters. A song of marriage is sung and then Rosalind – no longer in disguise – offers herself first to her father and then to Orlando, her future husband. Phebe, of course, is mortified to discover that her Ganymede is really a woman. Hymen intervenes and joins Orlando to Rosalind, Oliver to Celia, Silvius to Phebe and, last and perhaps least, Touchstone to Audrey. A further song concludes the wedding ceremony. The Duke welcomes the company. Phebe promises to love Silvius. Then, suddenly, a messenger arrives. He is another Jaques, the middle brother of Orlando and Oliver. He tells how Duke Frederick, hearing that many young men have come to join Duke Senior in his exile, has vowed to ride out and kill them. However, at the edge of the forest the wicked Duke met a hermit, who converted him to a holy life. Duke Frederick has resigned his usurped kingdom to his brother and restored all the lands he has seized to the nobles. He will live out the remainder of his life as a hermit. Duke Senior welcomes the news, but declares that the whole party should fall to enjoying some 'rustic revelry' before returning to their rightful places in the dukedom. He is about to lead the party off when the melancholy Jaques, hearing of Duke Frederick's conversion to a hermit's life, vows to follow him. No one can dissuade Jaques, but, before he goes, he wishes joy to the Duke, Oliver, Orlando and Silvius. But he tells Touchstone that his marriage will last for only two months. A slight note of bitterness prevents the end of the play from being too sentimental. When Touchstone has left, the Duke ushers the party off the stage, and only Rosalind is left to break the dramatic illusion and step forward to speak the Epilogue.

Scene by Scene Analysis

ACT I SCENE i

We are introduced to Orlando, the hero of the play. He is bewailing his fortunes to Adam, an old retainer. In this way, Shakespeare manages to convey to his audience the information they need to know. We learn, for example, that Orlando's father is dead, that he is a younger son, that his inheritance is small and that his older brother – whose name we later learn is Oliver – has neglected his education. This last point seems particularly unfair in view of the fact that another brother, called Jaques (who is not to be confused with the 'melancholy Jaques' of the later scenes), has been well taught. We begin to suspect that Oliver has a profound, irrational dislike of Orlando and takes every opportunity of humiliating him. Orlando then goes on to declare that he is worse provided for than Oliver's horses. They are properly trained, while he is not. He makes the strong but irrational dislike his brother has for him yet more apparent (ll. 15–19). Such a life as he is forced to live, Orlando declares, grieves him. He 'begins to mutiny against this servitude'. He adds, moreover, that the spirit of his father is working inside him to make him angry in this way. For the moment, however, he has no idea what to do.

You should notice how Shakespeare introduces his hero. Here is a young and clearly attractive man for whom we at once feel sorry. Our appreciation of Orlando is enhanced by his desire to do something about his plight, but we should be aware of how, right at the start, Shakespeare has introduced us not just to his hero, but to the themes of injustice and brotherly hatred that will be important to the whole play. One further point should also be noticed. It concerns stagecraft. Although Orlando is apparently talking to Adam, the old servant

already knows the facts of Orlando's case. The real purpose of the
speech is to provide the audience with an idea of Orlando's character
and some necessary information concerning his background. It is all
highly artificial. At first this may seem an example of weak technique.
After all, the situation is barely credible. You don't usually tell people
at length what they already know. But we should be careful. The sort
of comedy that Shakespeare is writing in this play *is* highly artificial.
That is part of its delight. Here, from the very beginning, Shakespeare
makes us aware of just this.

Adam sees Oliver coming (l. 24), and Orlando declares that when
they meet up it is certain there will be an argument. It breaks out at
once. Notice the curt, insolent tone of Oliver's questions. He is clearly
spoiling for a fight. Oliver is obviously a man of deep and irrational
hatred. He is a 'stage villain'. This is again part of the conventional,
artificial nature of the play. (You will find these matters discussed more
fully on pp. 33 and 84.)

As the argument proceeds, so Orlando's spirits become more ardent.
Challenged by Oliver, he stands his ground and declares that while
Oliver may be the oldest of the brothers, he, Orlando, is just as much
a son of their father. Convention may allow Oliver to be more respected
as the older brother, but that does not mean that Orlando is worthless.
Oliver is furious at this and begins to threaten Orlando, who, to protect
himself, seizes his brother by the throat. Oliver calls him a villain.
Orlando denies the charge. He states again that he is the worthy son
of a worthy father and that had not Oliver been of his own blood, he
would have pulled his tongue out. We see once more the fighting spirit
that is an important part of Orlando's character.

No notice is taken of the venerable Adam as he tries to part the
quarrelling brothers (ll. 59–60). Orlando refuses to let Oliver go
until he has told him to his face that Oliver has betrayed the trust
laid on him by his father to educate the young man. Orlando declares
that he has been brought up like a 'peasant' and that he has had
no chance to reveal his 'gentleman-like qualities'. He says for a
second time that the 'spirit' of his father is welling up inside him, and
demands that Oliver either educate him properly or give him the
small inheritance bequeathed him. Oliver sneers at this (l. 70) and
mutters ominously about not being troubled by his brother for much
longer. Clearly he has evil plans in mind. He orders Orlando to leave

him. He then calls Adam an 'old dog' and tells him to go with Orlando.

Adam – the faithful old retainer – is disturbed by Oliver's tone. Is this the reward for his years of loyal service? The boys' father would never have behaved like this. The old rule of kind authority has clearly been broken, and, as we shall see, this is a theme that is frequently taken up in the early part of the play.

Left on his own, Oliver makes his hatred for his brother clearer and vows to 'physic' him and deny him his inheritance. Clearly, he wants to have Orlando removed, and he calls for Dennis, one of his servants. When he enters, Oliver makes inquiries about Charles, the Duke's wrestler. He is told that the man is waiting to see him. Plans clarify in the wicked brother's mind. He hints darkly that the wrestling match will serve his purpose well.

Charles enters (l. 90). Since the audience require further information to enable them to understand the plot, the conversation between Charles and Oliver – just like the one at the start of the play – is designed to provide them with this. We learn, for example, that the old Duke of the country has been banished by the younger Duke Frederick. This is another example of brotherly hatred. We are further told that the older Duke has fled to the Forest of Arden and that 'three or four loving lords' have gone into voluntary exile with him. There they live 'like the old Robin Hood of England'. Many more young men are flocking to join them (alert members of the audience might suspect that Orlando will become one of them), and the wrestler then declares that their life is an idyllic one. The lords 'fleet the time carelessly as they did in the golden world'. This is the first hint of something very important to the play: the ideal life of country happiness. This form of existence we call 'pastoral'. Like much else in the play, it is both delightful and highly artificial. You will find the idea of 'pastoral' discussed more fully on pp. 33 and 84–7. Here we should see that it forms a pleasant contrast to the world of hatred we have met in the court. That the real pastoral life is not all a delightful idyll is something we shall see Shakespeare discussing later.

The conversation between Oliver and Charles also introduces us to the heroine of the play. We learn that the older, banished Duke has a daughter called Rosalind. She has not gone into exile with her father, but has stayed in the court of the younger Duke, the usurper, because of her friendship with that man's daughter, a girl who we shall learn is called Celia. Here is something to contrast with the brotherly hatreds we have seen so far: two girls, cousins to each other, staying close by each other's side in times of hardship. Apart from Adam's loyalty, it is the first example of real affection between living people that we have so far come across in the play. And it is just such moods of affection as these that will swell into the great theme of love on which the play is constructed.

Oliver now asks Charles if he is to wrestle before 'the new Duke' tomorrow. Charles says that he is to do so and tells Oliver that he has been given 'secretly to understand' that no lesser man than Orlando himself is going to 'try a fall' against him. This puts Charles in a difficult position. He is to wrestle tomorrow for his own reputation: to enhance his credit, in other words. This means that he cannot make allowances for any of the competitors. He must defeat each of them, and defeat means broken limbs for the loser. Charles knows that Orlando is 'young and tender', and he is loath to hurt him. This he thinks he must do if the young man comes to fight him. Because Charles has a high respect for Oliver, he has come to ask him either to dissuade his younger brother from wrestling or to warn him of the 'disgrace' that will attend what Charles sees as Orlando's inevitable defeat.

Again, the whole situation could hardly be more contrived. It fits in with Oliver's evil plans perfectly. He now begins to unfold these. He tells Charles quite untruthfully that he has already tried to dissuade Orlando from fighting, but to no effect (ll. 129–130). He then proceeds to blacken Orlando's character. He tells Charles that Orlando is stubborn, vicious and 'a secret and villainous contriver against me, his natural brother'. The truth, of course, is just the reverse. However, Oliver is clearly an accomplished liar and he begins to persuade Charles that it would be a very good thing if the wrestler did break Orlando's neck. If he does not do so, Oliver adds, it is quite likely that Orlando will find some 'treacherous device' to take the wrestler's life. Now that he is confident that he has persuaded Charles, Oliver's hypocrisy and melodramatic nature become blatant. He says that it is 'almost with tears' that he is forced to describe his younger brother as the most villainous young man of his day. To analyse his faults ('anatomize' him, l. 145) would make him blush and weep, while Charles himself would 'look pale and wonder'. This is the stuff of the villains of melodrama. Shakespeare, of course, was perfectly aware that such overstatement as Oliver's easily becomes comic. It is part of his purpose to make us laugh. Oliver's character is an aspect of Shakespeare's concern with artificial effects. You should notice how he uses the word 'brotherly' in line 145 in an ironic way. Clearly, we are to be amused by the unnaturalness of Oliver even while we see his evil in action.

Charles is very glad to have been told all this about Orlando. He vows to 'give him his payment'. In other words, he will defeat him in the wrestling match. Charles leaves, highly delighted that he can be of such service.

Oliver, left alone, confesses his deep and irrational hatred for Orlando in a soliloquy. He does not know why he hates Orlando so greatly. He only knows that he does so. He recognizes that there is no justification for his feelings. He reports that Orlando is a gentleman, learned (despite being deprived of education) and widely loved, especially by the servants. Oliver feels that he almost pales into insignificance beside him. However, 'it shall not be so long; this wrestler shall clear all'. Oliver exits, vowing to make sure that Orlando will enter the fight. That Orlando might win never occurs to him.

ACT I SCENE ii

Here we meet the two heroines of the play: Rosalind, the daughter of the older and banished Duke, and her cousin, Celia. You should note that this – like many other scenes in the play – is rich in puns and word-play. This again is part of Shakespeare's comic and artificial effect. It serves to emphasize the quick-wittedness of the two girls, Rosalind in particular, and so is an important part of her character (see pp. 61–9). It is absolutely essential that you pay close attention to the notes on this scene. You *must* understand the puns if you are fully to appreciate the play. Your Penguin edition gives a full account of these.

We find Celia trying to cheer Rosalind, who, very naturally, is depressed by memories of her father. Celia tries to rally her by saying that if Rosalind really loved her, then she would take Celia's father for her own. Celia herself would do this if she were in Rosalind's position.

Besides, Celia is her father's only heir (l. 16) and, when he dies, she will give all her inheritance back to Rosalind, to whom, in truth, it really belongs.

You should notice that it is not the content of these arguments that cheers Rosalind so much as the effort Celia is making and Rosalind's own natural good spirits. Throughout much of the rest of the play, high spirits will be a distinguishing feature of Rosalind's character. They are part of her natural, life-loving vivacity. She thinks at once 'of falling in love'. Such intelligent, witty liveliness attracts us to her immediately.

Celia is less certain of the propriety of falling in love. Love should only be a 'sport', a joke. She suggests rather that they mock Fortune, whose turning wheel brings some people good things, others bad. Rosalind agrees that Fortune is particularly unfair to women. Celia adds that the beautiful ones do not live 'honest' lives, while the respectable ones are plain. Rosalind jibs at this, but their light-hearted argument is interrupted by the arrival of Touchstone.

Touchstone is a clown, a court jester. We need to know that such men, dressed in the patched coat that was the sign of their trade, were regularly employed in large houses. Their function was to entertain with jokes, songs and witticisms. Such figures occur frequently in Shakespeare's plays. We find them in *Twelfth Night* and *King Lear*, for example. Shakespeare always uses them as figures who can tell the truth in a riddling but usually accurate way. The name 'Touchstone' is itself significant. A touchstone was the piece of finely grained stone which, it was believed, could test the value of gold and silver alloys. Just as such metals were rubbed against touchstones to test their worth, so the characters in *As You Like It* come into contact with Touchstone the clown to have their worth tested too. (Be sure to use your notes carefully so that you understand the very complex – if light-hearted – word-play between Rosalind and Celia in lines 42–54.)

Touchstone has come to tell Celia that her father has sent for her. A witty exchange takes place between him and the two girls, but you should notice how it modulates in Celia's speech at line 79 into something more serious. This again is typical of the varying range of moods in the play and is a crucial part of Shakespeare's dramatic effect. Notice too how Celia mentions the whip. Jesters who carried their jokes too far could be beaten. Touchstone says that it is a pity that fools cannot speak the truth when the so-called wise men act foolishly.

Le Beau, a singularly foolish courtier, now enters, full of gossip. He appears shallow and heartless. He tells the young ladies that they have 'lost much good sport'. The women tease Le Beau for his pompous airs and language. Eventually, he manages to tell them that they have missed the early bouts of the wrestling match and he begins to describe these. He tells how an old man and his three sons came to the ring and how each son has been so badly hurt by Charles that they are likely to die. Again, the tone of light-hearted mockery becomes serious. Notice how it is the lively Rosalind who says 'Alas!' Touchstone too is appalled. He doubts whether such wrestling is really suitable as a 'sport' for ladies. The note of sympathy we find here endears us to Touchstone as a feeling man, despite his fool's costume.

Nevertheless, Rosalind is keen to see the rest of the match, and, as Le Beau has already told us, the ring is to be brought on stage. At this moment, Duke Frederick (Celia's father) enters with his court, Orlando and Charles, the wrestler.

Duke Frederick declares that he has tried to dissuade Orlando from fighting, but to no effect. Celia's sympathy immediately goes out to the young man. Duke Frederick tells the girls that they will take little delight in the wrestling bout, for the odds against Orlando seem so great. He begs them to try and dissuade Orlando from fighting. Le Beau calls Orlando over. The hero and heroine of the play are about to meet.

Rosalind questions Orlando, while Celia tries to dissuade him as her father had asked her to. Rosalind urges the same course. Orlando will not lose his reputation if he bows out. They will see to that. But Orlando is adamant. Much as he is reluctant to deny the ladies anything – his gentlemanly manners become evident here – he must fight. He asks the young ladies to wish him well, declaring that, after all, he has nothing to lose. He does not care if he is killed. There is no one to mourn for him. He has nothing in the world. He may as well leave his place in it and have it filled by another.

Rosalind is touched. She wishes this unhappy and dispossessed young man – whose plight surely reminds her of her own – all the 'little strength' she has to give him. In such a way Rosalind suggests the first stirrings of her affection for Orlando.

Charles summons Orlando to the ring, implying as he does so that his death is imminent. Duke Frederick declares that the two men shall try only one fall. Charles boasts that this will be quite enough. The wrestling then begins. Here – if we are only reading the play – we must use our visual imagination. We should picture the two men preparing, their first grip on each other, the rising excitement of the girls as Orlando begins to show his reserves of strength, gains his advantage and, finally, throws Charles. It is particularly important that we *do* picture the whole scene in our imagination, for not only does it show us the reason for Rosalind's intense excitement at Orlando's victory – and hence the burgeoning of her love – but also it has a most important part to play in the presentation of Orlando himself. It establishes that he is strong and manly. It is just this impression which we will need to bear in mind as we see him fall in love. His later behaviour as a lover – which is certainly meant to amuse us – could suggest that Orlando is a rather feeble character. Quite the reverse is true. The wrestling match shows us that it is indeed a virile young man who becomes so smitten with passion. Orlando is neither feeble nor wholly self-indulgent.

The speechless Charles – the sometime boasting wrestler – is carried out. So much, we may say, for the villainous Oliver's attempt to have his brother removed.

Duke Frederick comes to speak to the victorious Orlando and, when he has discovered his name, again shows that rapid shift to doubt and melancholy which is a characteristic of the whole play. Orlando's father, whom we know already to have been a worthy old man, was an enemy of the usurper Duke Frederick. The memory of him – the memory of the virtue which Duke Frederick has successfully connived against – is enough to send him reluctantly away. The court exits, leaving Rosalind, Orlando and Celia on stage together.

Celia is disturbed by her father's behaviour. Orlando declares his pride in his father, and Rosalind declares that her father – the banished Duke – loved old Sir Rowland de Boys 'as his soul', and that the whole world agreed with him. Clearly, wicked men have usurped all the influence in the land.

Celia urges that they go and talk further with Orlando. She is obviously deeply troubled by her father's behaviour and she is also keen to praise Orlando for his bravery. Rosalind, evidently deeply in love – quietly, sadly and perhaps with slight embarrassment at the growing power of her feelings – gives Orlando a gold chain. Then she begins to leave. Orlando calls out his thanks in a touchingly modest speech. Rosalind immediately wants to turn back: 'Did you call, sir?' She begins to confess that she is in love. Orlando has not only 'overthrown' Charles, he has also won a victory over her heart. Celia – embarrassed, perhaps – bids Rosalind leave with her.

Orlando, left alone, realizes that he too has fallen in love. He also has been 'overthrown'.

Le Beau enters. As so frequently happens in the play, a note of joy is immediately changed to one of fear and dark suspicion. Duke Frederick, as Le Beau declares, is 'humorous' – in other words, he is subject to quickly changing moods. His temper now is all suspicion. He 'misconsters', or misconstrues, all that Orlando has done. It would be better for Orlando to leave at once. Orlando thanks Le Beau and asks which of the two girls was the Duke's daughter.

We are used to somewhat ridiculous pretentiousness in Le Beau's words, but his speech beginning at line 260 in fact says something important: Celia (here described as the taller of the two girls, but see p. 32) is Duke Frederick's daughter, but her 'manners' are so different from his that she hardly appears to be his daughter at all. Le Beau then explains both girls' parentage and the great love that exists between them. Far more significantly, he tells us that Duke Frederick has also taken against Rosalind for no other reason than that the people love her and pity her because of what has happened to her father. Le Beau warns Orlando that his malice 'will suddenly break forth'. Here, once again, is that tone of deep, irrational hatred that marks the early part of the play. Le Beau leaves, wishing to meet Orlando again 'in a better world than this'. His last words show his respect for Orlando. Le Beau is perhaps not quite so shallow as he at first appeared.

ACT I SCENE iii

Rosalind's melancholy mood, we discover (l. 19), is a result of her new feelings of love for Orlando. Celia once again tries to joke her out of her sadness, but to no effect. Can Rosalind, she asks, really have fallen in love with Orlando so suddenly (l. 26)? Rosalind does not answer

directly, and the girls' conversation is interrupted by the arrival of
Duke Frederick. The 'humorous' mood that Le Beau had warned of
has turned suddenly to open hatred of Rosalind. His eyes are 'full of
anger'. He orders Rosalind to leave the court at once. If she is found
within twenty miles of it, she will be summarily executed. Rosalind
begs to be told what offence she has committed. She is sure that she
has never so much as wished him harm. Duke Frederick's answer is an
expression of his purely arbitrary and tyrannical nature: 'Let it suffice
thee that I trust thee not'. As Rosalind retorts, this is hardly a sufficient
reason for ordering her banishment. Duke Frederick's reply (l. 56) is
again an expression of a tyrant's hatred and fear of virtuous people.
Treason, Rosalind declares, is not an inherited disease. Besides, her
father was not a traitor (he is, we remember, the rightful Duke who
has been usurped). Celia then tries to beg for mercy. Her father
declares that it was only for her sake that Rosalind was not banished
earlier. Rosalind had initially been allowed to stay because the Duke
wished her to. Now Celia is old enough to appreciate Rosalind's true
worth and she can say that, if Rosalind is a traitor, then so is she. She
concludes her speech with a moving account of the friendship between
Rosalind and herself.

   Duke Frederick tries to warn Celia of the danger he believes that
Rosalind poses to her reputation. Again, these are the poisonous and
suspicious words of a tyrant. Rosalind, he says, is so virtuous that the
people pity and love her. The affection she wins 'robs' Celia of the
admiration that should be her own. To allow Rosalind to get away with
this shows Celia to be merely a 'fool'. How much more virtuous will
Celia seem when there is no Rosalind to dim her splendour. Duke
Frederick tells his daughter not to beg for mercy for her friend.
Rosalind is banished. Celia, horror-struck, declares that she too is
banished. Again, her father calls her a fool and repeats his sentence of
banishment on Rosalind. With this he leaves.

   The girls are left on their own. Celia's pity for Rosalind is clear, and
she bravely repeats that since her father has banished Rosalind, then
he has banished her too. Rosalind's grief is at first too great for her to
believe what Celia says, but Celia's affectionate and vigorous speech
in lines 94–103 convinces her. Does Rosalind not realize that Celia
loves her so much that they are one and the same person? They cannot
be parted. They must plan how they both will flee, where they will go,

what they will take. Celia's loyalty and loving enthusiasm here overflow and she succeeds in winning Rosalind to her plan.

Again, of course, the whole situation is wildly improbable, but this is part of the pastoral convention (see pp. 33, 84–7) which we have learned to accept.

Rosalind asks where they should go. Inevitably, Celia suggests they run off to the Forest of Arden and there seek out Rosalind's father. More immediately practical, Rosalind warns of the danger they would put themselves in. Celia at once suggests disguise. She will dress herself poorly and 'smirch' her face. The Duke's daughter will look like any ordinary working girl. At this, Rosalind's imagination kindles. Here is another revelation of that bright and healthy strength of spirit, wit and resilience that make her so attractive a figure. Rosalind suggests that she dress like a young man and present the world 'a swashing and a martial outside'.

Two points should concern us here. The first, and less important one, is an obvious inconsistency in the text. Le Beau declares (I, ii, 261) that Celia is the taller of the two girls. Here, Rosalind claims that she is the taller. The most likely explanation of this is that at some time between two performances the boy actors playing the parts of the two girls were changed and the text was imperfectly altered to account for their different statures. But this inconsistency is far less important than the idea of disguise, for, by changing their appearance in this way, by Rosalind's seeming to be a man while actually being a woman (and, at that, a woman played by a boy actor) Shakespeare introduces us to one of his most often used themes: the idea of illusion and reality, that what things seem to be is not always what they really are. This idea is of the greatest importance to *As You Like It* and is discussed more fully on pp 84–6.

To suit their new appearances, the girls also change their names. Rosalind will be called Ganymede and Celia Aliena – 'the exiled lady'. Then, with a flourish, Rosalind suggests they take Touchstone and their jewels with them. Thus prepared, they will fly away (l. 136):

To liberty, and not to banishment.

ACT II SCENE i

We now enter the idyllic, pastoral world of the Forest of Arden.
Pastoral was a favourite 'convention' of the Elizabethans. What do we
mean by this? It may be helpful if we think of a modern bookshop or
library. Some shelves will contain spy stories, some detective novels,
others will display romantic fiction. In each case, we know roughly
what sort of story we can expect from each of these divisions. They
follow their own conventions, we say. From spy stories we expect a fast-
moving and complicated plot full of carefully researched detail. In the
more old-fashioned form of detective novel we expect all the characters
to gather at the end and for the detective to brilliantly unravel the steps
that led to the most unlikely of the suspects committing the crime.
These are the 'conventions' of each form. It is just so with the 'pastoral
convention'. We expect princes and princesses in disguise, delightful
and innocent rustic peasants, strange and sudden reverses of fortune
and, above all, love. *As You Like It* has its full measure of all these.
But it also does something else. Unless they are kept bright, conventions can quickly become very banal. The princes and princesses
of pastoral can lose contact with any semblance of life. The rustics can
be too good to be true. The adventures can become monotonous. Love
can become just a matter of clichés. Most important of all, perhaps,
the idea that the countryside is endlessly charming is not really true
at all. The never-never-land of pastoral can become thin and sentimental. Shakespeare was fully aware of this, and we shall see that
throughout *As You Like It* he constantly tests the conventions. Sometimes he makes us smile at them, at other times he makes us realize
that the real countryside – the Forest of Arden around Stratford, for
example – can be cruel, tiring and difficult to live in. In this way
Shakespeare makes the conventions alive and requires his audience to
keep their wits about them.

Rosalind's father, Duke Senior, opens the second act with a
famous account of the delights of the pastoral life. He and his fellows
have left the 'painted pomp' of the court. Their exile is 'sweet'.
None of them, he says, feel 'the penalty of Adam'. In other words,
this is a land where it is for ever spring. Even the wind (which for
all the Duke's praises of the woodland life *is* clearly uncomfortable)
teaches him a lesson in morality. Indeed, as the following lines make

clear, everything in the Forest of Arden is a lesson in virtue
(ll. 12–17):

> *Sweet are the uses of adversity,*
> *Which, like the toad, ugly and venomous,*
> *Wears yet a precious jewel in his head;*
> *And this our life, exempt from public haunt,*
> *Finds tongues in trees, books in the running brooks,*
> *Sermons in stones, and good in everything.*

You should notice that the tone of this speech is neither simple nor
straightforward. By the close of it we feel, perhaps, that the Duke is
being rather over-enthusiastic, a little false. Furthermore, although he
is keen to praise the delights of country existence, it is not really quite
as perfect a form of life as he would wish. It may well be springtime,
but no one can escape 'the penalty of Adam'. The wind in fact does
blow. Indeed, it has an 'icy fang'. The Duke shrinks with cold.
Adversity is an ugly toad, for all that he 'wears ... a precious jewel in
his head'. These apparent contradictions – the proper critical word is
'ambiguity' – are an important part of *As You Like It* and a full and
proper reading of the play will be alert to them. They are a crucial part
of Shakespeare's technique of simultaneously using the pastoral convention and testing out its truth.

Amiens compliments the Duke on his ability to see the 'sweet' side
of his misfortunes. The Duke then declares that they should go
hunting. Again, there is an ambiguity here. By going hunting the
courtiers are bringing death to the deer, the 'native burghers' of the
forest. The Duke recognizes an element of cruelty in this, and the First
Lord's reply is an interesting one. We have just seen the Duke moralizing about the country life. Everything in Arden serves as a lesson on
right living. But there is another courtier who is particularly prone to
finding 'tongues in trees, books in the running brooks'. This man is 'the
melancholy Jaques'. Clearly, the philosopher is an object of some
amusement to the court wits. The First Lord describes how they crept
up behind Jaques as he watched the death of a stag. (Notice the
combination of amusement, pity and suffering in the description of the
stag's death. It is a further example of ambiguity.) Jaques at once began
to 'moralize this spectacle'. For him, everything in the forest is to be
read as a satire on human folly. Human folly, as we shall see, is what

Jaques intends to expose throughout the course of the play. The tears of the stag falling into the river suggest to him how humans give to those who already have enough. When the dying stag withdraws, it reminds Jaques of how the wretched go off on their own. The herd of deer that then sweeps by becomes, in Jaques's eyes, the herd of ordinary citizens. Clearly, Jaques is, in the First Lord's opinion, a ridiculous figure who thoroughly enjoys being bitter at everyone else's expense. And it is right to see this absurd side to Jaques's personality.

But the man is by no means foolish. The point that he makes about the Duke's court usurping the kingdom of the deer and bringing fear and death to it has a point. The issue had worried the Duke himself. Jaques is clearly a figure of whom we should take some notice, even while we smile at him. Here is ambiguity at the very heart of one of the characters in the play. Notice too how the First Lord's vivid description of his 'weeping and commenting' on the deer rouses our interest in the man. We have not met him yet, but we strongly want to. So does the Duke. He wants to be entertained by Jaques. The First Lord obediently goes to fetch him.

ACT II SCENE ii

This short scene has two main purposes: it contrasts the cruel world of the court with the pastoral idyll we have just seen; and it provides us with some necessary information. Rosalind and Celia have left the court and taken Touchstone with them. The Second Lord also re-tells an item of court gossip. It is now known that Rosalind and Celia are interested in Orlando, and it is believed that the young man will be found in the ladies' company. The furious Duke Frederick orders Oliver to be brought before him. Oliver must seek them out. All efforts must be made to find the 'foolish runaways'.

ACT II SCENE iii

In fact, Orlando is not with the girls. He has returned home after the wrestling match. Oliver, of course, had hoped that the wrestling would be the end of Orlando. However, since Charles was the one who was worsted, Oliver has now to take matters into his own hands. Old Adam greets Orlando and is barely able to tell him what Oliver has planned.

Adam's long speech is again not without its ambiguities. We know him to be a thoroughly worthy old man, and this aspect of Adam's character will be most touchingly developed in the following lines. But he is also comicly rambling in his speech here. It is quite impossible for Orlando to grasp what he is trying to say. Adam (partly, of course, to stress these ideas in the audience's mind) emphasizes Orlando's worth, the fact that he is strong, lovable and, most importantly, a part of the old and virtuous world of his father that has now been so brutally replaced both at home and in the court.

All that Orlando can at present derive from the old man's rambling is that he is in some sort of danger. He asks what the matter is. Adam is so horrified by what he has to tell that again he cannot express himself directly. He eventually manages to tell Orlando that his brother means to burn him alive or kill him in whatever way he can. Orlando must at all costs flee. The young man asks where he can go and, since he has no money, how he can support himself. Must he become a beggar or a highwayman? Such a life he refuses out of hand (ll. 35–7). He would prefer to face his brother.

A moment of great tenderness follows: a moment of love, selflessness and great dignity, which it is important to remember. It is one of the series of very moving moments in this comedy. Adam offers Orlando his lifetime's savings. He offers to the young man what he has put by for his own old age, the time when he will be lame and an example of 'unregarded age in corners thrown'. The phrase is an example of the vivid and accurately observed detail of harsh everyday life which keeps the play so emotionally various. God, declares Adam, must look after him now. He begs Orlando to take him along as his servant. Again, the sense of trust and loyalty here is of the greatest importance. These are true and honest values. Orlando is deeply touched by them and by Adam's suggestion of 'the constant service of the antique world'. This, of course, is part of the play's discussion of real love and genuine feeling. These are matters that will be constantly tested. We have seen already how they have been lost both in the court and in Orlando's own home. We have watched Duke Senior finding morality in the Forest of Arden. We have heard how Jaques castigates vice. Here, by contrast, is virtue in action: loyalty, service, the health that comes from an honest life.

Orlando is deeply touched by Adam's generous offer. He recognizes that the old retainer is not like the corrupt modern world. He makes it clear, however, that he can do nothing in return for Adam's gift (ll. 63–5). Nevertheless, he decides to flee and to take the old man with him. He promises that they will find 'some settled low content' before they have run through all his money. With an expression of sadness and intense loyalty from Adam, the two men, young and old, set off.

ACT II SCENE iv

The runaways from Duke Frederick's court are exhausted. Indeed, Rosalind is so tired that she could almost cry (l. 5). Only her disguise makes her behave like the man she is pretending to be. We learn that they have now reached the Forest of Arden. Touchstone declares that he was better off at home. Their first experience of the pastoral world is not a very heartening one.

But the pastoral world is not without its amusements. As the travellers rest, Corin and Silvius enter. Silvius, the younger of the two, is deeply in love. Love, of course, was supposed to be a principal occupation of young shepherds, and Shakespeare has great delight here in ridiculing the conventional excesses of such passion. The effect – which can only really be appreciated in the theatre – is superbly comic. We must suppose that both Corin and Silvius have thick rustic accents. When Silvius begins to sigh out his love in an unintentional parody of the sophisticated poetry of the time, this ambiguity is wonderfully effective. It is another example of the rich variety of language in Shakespeare's text.

Silvius's love for Phebe has totally overwhelmed him. He is in the grip of a passion that draws him to 'many actions most ridiculous'. He knows that his behaviour is skittish, absurd and just what a lover's should be. Calling desperately after his mistress, he breaks 'from company' and dashes away.

Extreme passion such as this is clearly not without its ludicrous side. This is a central idea in the play. Love can make all of us act like fools, and almost no one in the play is immune to such behaviour. But, for all its absurdity, love can be both a painful and a serious matter. Silvius's behaviour has reminded Rosalind of her own feelings (ll. 40–41), and even Touchstone remembers his experiences of love. Not for him – now, or in the future – is the refined and extreme ardour we have just been witnessing. Touchstone's love for Jane Smile – like his later love for Audrey – is far more down to earth and charmingly physical. But it is also, in its way, equally absurd. There are some beautifully acute memories in Touchstone's speech, and he too realizes that (ll. 49–51):

We that are true lovers run into strange capers; but as all is mortal in nature, so is all nature in love mortal in folly.

This is a shrewd comment, and it tells us a great deal about the play. Rosalind herself fully appreciates Touchstone's insight.

Celia, who has, it seems, no memories of love to call on, returns us to the world of reality. She is hungry, and she asks Touchstone to speak to Corin and beg him for food.

What follows is delightful. Touchstone is very much the courtly man who would make fun of the local peasants. He is so absurdly condescending to Corin that Rosalind is embarrassed by his behaviour. Corin, however, is not over-impressed. The trio of courtiers looks 'very wretched' to him. At this point Rosalind takes the initiative and asks Corin for help in a decent and straightforward way. Once more, Corin's reply shows that the pastoral world is far from being always idyllic. Corin has a low place in country society. He does not own his own property, but is 'shepherd to another man' – a cruel and hard man, as it appears. Corin informs Rosalind that this man's goods are all up for sale at the moment. Corin has virtually nothing to eat or to live on. Nonetheless, with true charity he welcomes the travellers to share what there is. The notes of kindliness and hardship – themes which appear throughout the play – are sounded here.

The fact that the property on which Corin works is up for sale suggests to Rosalind that she should ask who the person is who is going to buy it. The young Silvius apparently wishes to own it, but in his present state of passion he 'little cares for buying anything'. Rosalind at once shows that intuitive and lively generosity that is so important a part of her character. She suggests the shepherd buy the property with their money. Celia adds that they will willingly employ him. She has begun to grow fond of the pastoral world and, in proper pastoral fashion, she, Rosalind and Touchstone will set up as shepherds. Corin is delighted by the sudden change in his fortunes. We have seen that such changes are an aspect of the pastoral convention. He leads the travellers away so that they can find out more about the farm and decide whether they really want it. He then promises to be their faithful servant.

ACT II SCENE v

The scene opens with a stanza from one of Shakespeare's most famous songs. Among the audience is Jaques. As the stanza comes to an end, he asks for more. Amiens teases him about its making him melancholy, but in his reply Jaques exposes himself as the perfect type of the melancholy man (ll. 11–12). You will find a fuller discussion of this very important aspect of Jaques's personality on pp. 72–4 and 88–9. Here, meanwhile, as the scene develops, we notice both his exaggerated dislike of the world and his ability to make sharp comments. Clearly, he considers the world to be entirely populated by fools.

ACT II SCENE vi

But if there is foolishness and affectation in the world, then there is also suffering and genuine compassion. Old Adam, for all his vaunted good health, is exhausted, starving and near to death. Orlando tries to comfort him and vows to find him food and return with it. This short, touching scene – which prepares us for the climax of the next scene – ends with Orlando carrying the old man off to shelter.

ACT II SCENE vii

This is one of the great scenes in the play and contains one of the most famous speeches in all of Shakespeare's work. It serves both to display the character of Jaques and to underline the limited nature of his powerfully expressed ideas.

The Duke is again requesting Jaques's company. Jaques enters and, amazingly, he is laughing. He has met Touchstone, a genuine fool, and listened to him while he 'railed on Lady Fortune'. Touchstone's trite and comic moralizing appeals to Jacques deeply. The idea of a moral fool so delights him that (ll. 30–33):

> *My lungs began to crow like Chanticleer*
> *That fools should be so deep-contemplative;*
> *And I did laugh, sans intermission,*
> *An hour by his dial.*

Jaques now longs to be a fool in his motley coat himself. His imagination has been kindled by what he thinks is Touchstone's idiotic behaviour. He too would like the fool's liberty 'to blow on whom I please', to rail and satirize men who cannot, without exposing their folly even more, retort to his attacks (ll. 53–7). The fool's gown is just the thing for Jaques to wear while he pursues his ambition to 'cleanse the foul body of th'infected world'.

The Duke is more suspicious of Jaques's claims to virtue. He knows well that, in his time, Jaques has been a 'libertine', a loose-living and immoral man. Jaques, in lines 70–87, gives a satirist's usual form of defence. When he rails at pride or vanity or whatever, he is not being personally spiteful, he is not attacking any particular man or woman. Rather, he is indicating the general and widespread nature of each vice. This should make each man examine his own behaviour thoroughly. If the criticism applies to any such man, then Jaques's comments should help him reform his behaviour. If the criticisms do not apply, then Jaques has done no harm.

Orlando enters. He is violent and desperate. He must have food for Adam. The self-indulgence of Jaques is suddenly cut short. The Duke asks Orlando what is the matter. Is Orlando truly desperate or just 'a rude despiser of good manners'? Orlando declares himself to be a truly desperate man. He will kill any of the courtiers who touch the food before them until he has what he wants. The Duke bids Orlando join them. Orlando is surprised by his courtesy. He had thought that all the living creatures in the forest would be savage. Instead, he has found politeness. Blushing, he puts away his sword (l. 120). The Duke confesses that indeed he and his men, as Orlando has suggested, have seen 'better days'. They know politeness, and therefore the Duke again bids Orlando join them. The young man confesses that he has another to look after (ll. 128–30). When he has described Adam and his suffering, the Duke bids him go and bring the old man to the feast. As Orlando goes, Duke Senior again indulges his taste for moralizing. The world is a theatre, he says, and presents 'more woeful pageants' than the one in which they are obliged to act.

To Jaques, such melancholy reflections are irresistible. They call forth his finest poetry, one of the most famous speeches in world theatre: 'The Seven Ages of Man'. This is a wonderful piece of rhetoric, of words patterned and shaped into the most convincing of forms.

Jaques builds on the Duke's image of the world being a theatre to present a pageant of brief human life in seven acts. Each act – each age of man – has its pains, shortcomings and absurdities. Human ageing is also an inevitable decline into the dreadful picture of senility given at the close. The 'puking' baby, 'the whining schoolboy', the ridiculous lover, the bragging soldier, the self-important judge and sad old man all end in (ll. 166–7):

> *second childishness, and mere oblivion,*
> *Sans teeth, sans eyes, sans taste, sans everything.*

It is superb. It is vivid. But it is only partly true. Jaques has given a wonderfully powerful picture of human life which completely forgets charity and human dignity. Orlando now enters with Adam. We see youth caring for age and the Duke caring for both. Jaques's cynicism evaporates and he has nothing more to say in the whole scene.

The company eats while Amiens entertains them with a song. It too is bitter, a lyric about ingratitude. It forms an excellent contrast to the scene of generosity and concern that is played out before us. Here is yet another example of ambiguity: on the one hand, life is full of unkindness and deceit; on the other, it is full of trust and comradeship. It is with these contradictions that the act ends. Duke Senior recognizes Orlando as the true son of Sir Rowland de Boys, his friend. He welcomes Adam with an easy and natural charity. The company exits to hear the 'residue' of Orlando's story.

ACT III SCENE i

Duke Frederick has summoned Oliver to his presence. He demands that he seek out his brother, who, the Duke believes, is now in the company of Rosalind and Celia. You should notice how violent the Duke's feelings are. This is a tyrant's speech. He rounds on Oliver, telling him that if he does not find his brother 'within this twelve-month', then he too will be exiled and his lands confiscated until such time as he succeeds.

Oliver declares that he never loved his brother. The Duke declares that such unnatural behaviour shows Oliver to be a villain. He orders the immediate seizure of Oliver's property.

This short but harsh scene is a prelude to the amusing discussion of love, which is the main subject of Act III.

ACT III SCENE ii

The brother whom Oliver is to seek out is now far from the violent world of the court and its intrigues. He is in Arden and in love. Like Silvius, he is being drawn into 'many actions most ridiculous'. It is these that will serve as the basis of the comedy to come. We shall see that Shakespeare presents love as being both absurd and serious at one and the same time. Like all true pastoral lovers, Orlando has become a poet – a rather bad one. For the moment, he is pinning his verses on every tree. Rosalind, Celia and Touchstone, not to mention Jaques, will all find these poems an excuse for laughter. So will we. Here is the delightful, artificial world of pastoral love. As this scene progresses, so Shakespeare will develop this until love is seen in all its variety, charm and absurdity.

Touchstone enters with Corin. We have already seen (II, iv, 61–5) that Touchstone regards himself as a superior, witty man of the court set down amid a collection of country bumpkins. He is determined to get his full measure of enjoyment from this. To be sure, the clown is worldly-wise, but you should notice that Corin has a genuine natural nobility – a fine quality despite all Touchstone's attempts to put him down with his quicker wit.

Corin asks Touchstone how he likes the shepherd's life (l. 11). Touchstone's answer is a series of amusing paradoxes and contradictions. Such playing with words as this is a characteristic of the whole scene, and you should make sure that you really understand what is being said and appreciate the humour. Touchstone declares that the shepherd's life, while good in itself, is no sort of life at all. It is pleasantly secluded but too isolated, delightful in its open air appeal but 'tedious' because it is not the court. Such musings as Touchstone has here make him wonder if Corin has any philosophy of his own. In the pastoral convention (see pp. 33 and 84–7) shepherds were often regarded as being humble men who had fine and dignified ideas about life. Corin shows he has in a series of solid, common-sense statements that make him seem dull-witted, a 'natural' philosopher as Touchstone the clown calls him. In other words, Touchstone thinks Corin is a fool. Touchstone then begins to tease Corin, much to our amusement. He proceeds to prove to the simple rustic that he is 'damned' because he has never been in court. (Of course, it was the court life that was conventionally seen as being full of sin and therefore leading to damnation. The countryside was traditionally the place of virtue. Touchstone is turning ideas on their heads for our amusement.) Corin replies that some form of life suits the country, another the court. He is right, of course. Touchstone, however, gets the shepherd to support his allegations with examples. Touchstone wittily shows that each one of them completely contradicts what the shepherd wants to say. As Corin speaks, we feel he has a real, simple love for his way of life. We also appreciate Touchstone's quick-wittedness. This contrast is particularly clear in Corin's speech starting at line 69. The passage is a delightful invocation of the shepherd's honest life. It makes us feel the real attractions of country life. Touchstone's reply, which tries to suggest that man's forcing beast to mate is immoral, is witty.

The contest between these two is broken by Rosalind (still, of course, in her boy's disguise) entering with one of Orlando's poems. Touch-stone immediately offers a parody of it.

If you compare the two versions carefully (using your notes to help you), you will see that while Orlando's verses are full of pure, romantic adoration, Touchstone's parody recognizes the physical nature of love more frankly. Again, this is an aspect of the play that only a careful and delicate reading will bring out. But it is important. It is part of Shakespeare's mature and human view of love that it is both ideal and physical at the same time. *As You Like It* shows not only the absurd extremes of romantic adoration (especially in Silvius and Orlando), but also a knowledge of a more down-to-earth recognition of the body. Touchstone's affair with Audrey, for example, will express itself clearly in such terms. It is also part of Rosalind's charm that she frankly expresses both of these aspects of love too.

When Celia enters (l. 121), reading yet another of Orlando's poems, we see again how little skill this young poet really has. As Rosalind herself declares, the verses are a 'tedious homily'. But Celia wants to say more to Rosalind and to talk in private. She asks Touchstone and Corin to leave.

For a few moments the two girls make fun of the verses, but Celia then asks Rosalind if she knows who has written them. Rosalind confesses that she is very curious, but manages to convince Celia that she does not know who the poet is. Celia can barely believe this, and the spirits and excitement of both girls rise as their conversation edges inevitably towards mention of Orlando.

Shakespeare's effect here is quite a complex one, and it is particularly important to our understanding of Rosalind's character. Perhaps she genuinely does not know who the poet is. Perhaps she is just pretending not to know. Most likely of all, Rosalind knows who the poet is but does not dare to confess that she believes it to be the young Orlando. Remember how deeply in love she is. At the end of the wrestling match she confessed this. The sighs of young Silvius reminded her of how she felt. Now, as it becomes clear that her strong feelings are returned by Orlando, we sense her thrill with all the vigorous enthusiasm of young love. Look at her speech beginning at line 188. Listen to how the words tumble over each other in Rosalind's excitement. See too how Celia's words help to root the affair in common sense. Finally, when Celia has reaffirmed that the poet is indeed young Orlando

(l. 211), listen to the intense excitement into which Rosalind is thrown. Her obsession with Orlando spills out as a series of questions. But, underlying them, there is one great doubt (l. 222–3):

But doth he know that I am in this forest and in man's apparel?

The situation is highly artificial, highly ridiculous and wholly delightful. Such confusions and genuine feelings lie at the very heart of Shakespeare's comedy.

Rosalind's intense excitement is continued as she hears Celia describe how she found Orlando lying under a tree 'like a dropped acorn'. Indeed, Rosalind can barely restrain her excitement. Dressed as a boy though she is, her true instincts as a woman have been roused. As she so delightfully says (ll. 242–3):

Do you not know I am a woman? When I think, I must speak. Sweet, say on.

It is perfectly clear that Rosalind is head over heels in love.

At this moment Orlando himself comes by in the company of none other than the melancholy Jaques. The mock insults in their conversation give us an example of one of the sudden shifts of mood in the play, this time from Rosalind's rapture to Jaques's satire.

Jaques and Orlando, with great ironic civility, tell each other how they dislike each other's company. Jaques also tells Orlando that he thinks he has little talent as a poet (l. 252). Orlando answers to this and also to Jaques's taunts over Rosalind. His answers make the old man realize that Orlando has as keen a wit as he. Jaques admires this and suggests that Orlando join him in his favourite occupation: railing 'against our mistress the world'. But Orlando will have none of this. 'I am weary of you,' he says, and after a further exchange of banter Jaques leaves.

It is now Rosalind's turn to 'speak to him like a saucy lackey'. What follows is a dialogue of the greatest sophistication, wit and subtlety. It is not easy to understand, especially if we are following it on the page. Here, above all, it is essential to know the play from the theatre if we can. Only in this way can we truly appreciate the girl Rosalind (still dressed as a boy) looking at Orlando with the utmost fascination and being playfully abusive towards him even while she is trying to fascinate her young lover. We must feel how her inventive wit shows her love and high spirits, and we must also appreciate the delightful artificiality of the situation. Here is a young girl in love, dressed as a boy, Ganymede, taunting her lover who does not recognize her, and offering to cure him of his 'madness' if only he will pretend that she is his Rosalind 'and come every day to my cote, and woo me'.

Rosalind's bantering tone is clear from the start. Her quick-witted paradoxes (which, once more, you must make sure you properly understand by using the notes) capture Orlando's curiosity. He can scarcely believe that Ganymede with his quick wit and educated accent is a native of the forest. He seems, however, to accept his highly unlikely explanation (ll. 331–4) and to be interested in his story of how his 'old religious uncle' lectured him against love. Orlando begs him to say more, but Rosalind teasingly brings the conversation round to Orlando's poetry. 'If,' she says, 'I could meet that fancy-monger, I would give him good counsel.' Orlando confesses the truth at once. Rosalind, however, is still determined to tease him. She declares that Orlando has none of the signs of a true lover about him (ll. 358–68). Orlando, she says, is really only in love with himself. As we shall see, this is a shrewd comment. Orlando, however, insists that his passion is wholly for his Rosalind: 'Neither rhyme nor reason can express how much' (ll. 381–2).

Rosalind replies that she thinks love 'is merely a madness'. It deserves to be treated in the cruel way that the Elizabethans treated all insanity (ll. 383–7). This idea of a cure interests Orlando. Rosalind's reply is a delightfully satirical account of the absurdities and quickly changing moods of love that we have met before. Rosalind declares that she (in the guise of the boy Ganymede, of course) once cured a lover by having him pretend that she was his mistress. Ganymede then proved so difficult, so hard and contrary, that the madness of love was cured by driving the lover to the other insanity of religious isolation (ll. 400–402). Orlando states that such a course is not for him. For a moment it seems that Rosalind has overplayed her hand. Only a fine production in the theatre can show us the sense of pathos and love she reveals as she drops her voice and begins to woo Orlando afresh (ll. 407–8):

I would cure you, if you would but call me 'Rosalind', and come every day to my cote, and woo me.

Orlando agrees to this. The extravagant lover does not realize that in seeking a cure he is actually being wooed and won by the woman who loves him.

ACT III SCENE iii

Touchstone too has succumbed to the pastoral delights of love. However, as we might expect, he has not allowed himself to run to absurd extremes. Audrey – his chosen – is a simple country wench, and it is just her simplicity on which Touchstone exercises his wit. As they talk, the couple are watched by Jaques.

Again, the opening of this scene is constructed largely to show Touchstone's wit. As always, it is most important that you look at the notes thoroughly to make sure that you really understand what is being said. For example, what does the reference to Ovid in line 6 mean? Why is Jaques distressed that such knowledge should be in the possession of one so apparently low as Touchstone?

The discussion on poetry and 'feigning' that follows is a further example of Touchstone's delight in wit and paradox. The underlying idea here is that poetry is something 'made up', it is a fiction, a lie. Touchstone's jokes point to the fabrications that the extremes of romantic poetry require, while, at the same time, he makes fun of Audrey's simplicity. All of this delights Jaques's satirical nature.

But if Touchstone is being deliberately flippant in what he says, he also has a serious purpose in mind: he wants to get married. He has arranged that Sir Oliver Martext, 'the vicar of the next village', should perform the marriage ceremony (ll. 38–41). This, of course, is the first real mention of marriage in the play, and it is marriage that will be the inevitable happy end of all the other affairs we have been watching. Touchstone's, however, is rather rushed. For Touchstone and Audrey there is no long courtship or the exchange of fine and complex feelings. In this they are very different from Rosalind and Orlando. The needs of both Touchstone and Audrey are far more simple. Touchstone is a man of earthy passions which he wishes to slake. As he says later in the scene (ll. 72–4):

As the ox hath his bow, sir, the horse his curb, and the falcon her bells, so man hath his desires; and as pigeons bill, so wedlock would be nibbling.

Touchstone is sufficiently honourable to realize that he should get married before indulging his physical appetites, but his view of marriage is not a very exalted one. The complexities of his speech beginning at line 44 are meant to suggest this. The passage refers to horns (and hence to animals), and this not only suggests the physical excitement of sexuality but also refers to the belief that a cuckold (a man whose wife sleeps with other men) grows 'cuckold's horns' on his forehead. In other words, Touchstone sees marriage very much in terms of sex and of his wife's (and, presumably, his own) infidelities. This is a view of the relationship that Jaques will confirm right at the end of the play.

Sir Oliver Martext arrives and, when he realizes that there is no one to give Audrey away, Jaques emerges from his hiding place and offers to play the part. Nonetheless, he warns Touchstone that the foolish and illiterate Sir Oliver will make a botched job of the marriage. For Touchstone, this seems to be no real disadvantage (ll. 83–4):

. . not being well married, it will be a good excuse for me hereafter to leave my wife.

Jaques draws Touchstone to one side. Sir Oliver, however, is not to be tricked out of the fee he should get for performing the service, and he follows angrily after the lovers.

ACT III SCENE iv

For Rosalind, the course of true love is running far from smoothly. We move from mildly bawdy amusement to the spectacle of her suffering. Orlando is late for his appointment, and Rosalind has been thrown into an agony of doubt. She calls Orlando 'dissembling' (l. 6) and this suggests that he is shallow and lacks full-blooded passion (ll. 12–13). Celia loyally supports her friend and eventually tells her of Orlando's attending on 'the Duke your father'. Naturally, this raises a question in the mind of the attentive reader of the play. We know that both Rosalind and her father are in the Forest of Arden and yet they have not openly met. We learn that when Rosalind indeed saw her father yesterday she did not drop her disguise as Ganymede and, as a result, her father did not recognize her. Why should this be so? The reason is probably this: Shakespeare wants us to concentrate on Rosalind's relationship with Orlando. Even the mere suggestion of an open meeting between father and daughter would detract from the effect of this, and Shakespeare exploits the situation skilfully. 'But what talk we of fathers,' Rosalind says (ll. 34–5), 'when there is such a man as Orlando?' We feel that, while Rosalind may be a loyal daughter, the full force of her new love is much more important to her. Her concern for Orlando is the strongest thing in her life. It far outweighs her regard for her father. This, of course, is as it should be. Rosalind is eagerly and wholeheartedly committed to her love. But, as Celia points out, Orlando has failed to turn up. Probably, Celia says, Orlando is just a feeble and inconstant young man.

Corin now enters to divert the attention of the two women. He has seen poor suffering Silvius and his beloved Phebe. He promises Rosalind and Celia that if they will come and watch them, they will be richly rewarded with a delightful 'pageant' (or play) between the two young people. Silvius, as Corin says, is exhibiting 'the pale complexion of true love', while Phebe – who emerges as one of the most amusing characters in the play – shows him nothing but 'the red glow of scorn and proud disdain'.

Rosalind eagerly goes off to view this scene, promising also to 'prove a busy actor in their play'. However, things will not turn out quite as she expects.

ACT III SCENE v

This scene is a beautifully delicate satire on thwarted passion and cruel ladies. Remember, both the rustic characters are only simple peasants – their apparently sophisticated language and behaviour would be far more appropriate to members of courtly society.

When Rosalind, Celia and Corin enter, Silvius has just compared Phebe to an executioner. His language is fluently poetic and Phebe, realizing this, thinks, like Touchstone, that such emotions must be feigned. They are fictions. She bluntly and convincingly destroys the old cliché that one glance from her eye would cause Silvius to die. Her glances do not leave even the faintest trace on him, she says. Conventionally this is the sort of wit that we might expect from a great lady. It is delightfully comic when we hear it in Phebe's thick country accent.

Silvius then tells her that when Phebe in her turn falls in love, she will know how painful the experience is. Phebe says that she wants Silvius to stay away from her until that time comes. Rosalind then steps forward and – of course – Phebe believes her to be a boy and falls suddenly and deeply in love with her.

Rosalind's intention has been to put Phebe in her place. She now tells her that Phebe has no breeding, no good looks, and really nothing to recommend her at all. What reason has Phebe, then, to be so haughty (l. 40)? But Phebe has already fallen in love with her accuser and is staring at her in helpless adoration. Rosalind (dressed, of course, as Ganymede) refuses point-blank to be in the least affected by Phebe's stare. Rather, she is blisteringly insulting to her. She then turns on Silvius (l. 49). She tells him that he is a much better specimen of manhood than Phebe is of her own sex. Consequently, he is foolish to follow her so doggedly. Phebe is really rather ugly, and only because he loves her so hopelessly does she think that she is beautiful. Rosalind adds that the children of such an ill-matched pair can only be ugly in their turn. She then returns to Phebe (l. 57). Phebe, Rosalind says, should go down on her knees in gratitude to Silvius. After all, she is lucky to find anyone to love her at all. Rosalind advises her (l. 60):

> *Sell when you can, you are not for all markets.*

Evidently, Phebe has never been spoken to by a young man like this before. As a result, she finds Ganymede's scolding irresistibly exciting (l. 65):

> *I had rather hear you chide than this man woo.*

Rosalind realizes what has happened and also sees what she must do (ll. 66-9). Rebuffing Phebe in this way will be good fun.

Phebe and Silvius are then left alone. Both are now desperately in love. Silvius with Phebe, Phebe with Rosalind dressed as Ganymede. The absurdity of the situation is delightful. So is the way in which it develops.

Phebe now realizes that the hopelessly pining Silvius has his uses after all. Her brief replies to what he says at first suggest that Phebe is distracted by her new love, but, by line 92, she has recovered herself sufficiently to play the cruel (but this time calculating) lady. Because Silvius can 'talk of love so well', Phebe will use him to run messages to Ganymede for her (ll. 97–8):

> *But do not look for further recompense*
> *Than thine own gladness that thou art employed.*

Silvius is thrilled by the prospect.

Phebe's long speech beginning at line 109 is delightfully convincing. It is perfectly clear that she has fallen in love. She is trying to pretend to herself that this is not so, but she does not quite succeed. Her thoughts eddy back and forth. She wants to criticize Ganymede, but cannot bring herself to accept the criticisms she makes. She is annoyed by the fact that he is not more hurt by the tart comments he has received. In the end, she resolves to give as good as she has got. She will write to Ganymede what she considers to be 'a very taunting letter'. Silvius will deliver it. He agrees to do so, 'with all my heart'.

ACT IV SCENE i

Act IV opens with Jaques talking to Rosalind. She is quite a match for his wit, and is able to deflate the somewhat self-loving tone of his speech on his own melancholy that begins at line 10. Such is the spirited, intelligent and fascinating girl with whom Orlando has fallen in love. Orlando now enters, but, for some moments, he is not noticed by Rosalind, who busily continues making fun of Jaques. When she does finally turn to Orlando (l. 34), it is to tease him for his failing to come at the appointed time.

What follows is a scene that is both ridiculous and – on Rosalind's part, at least – full of the most deep and heart-felt feeling. We, as the audience, must bear both views constantly in mind. We have here a pair of lovers. Orlando, the young man, has convinced himself that he is desperately in love, and has been persuaded that what he believes to be another young man can cure him of his passions. He must pretend

paradox
ambiguity
absurdity

that this young man – Rosalind dressed as Ganymede – is indeed his own mistress and then willingly subject himself to the most contrary behaviour in the hope that he will eventually give up love altogether. So far, so absurd. But there is more. The 'boy' that Orlando is wooing – pretending that he is his girlfriend – really *is* his girlfriend. She, for her part, relying on her disguise as a boy, has convinced Orlando that she can cure him of his love. What Rosalind in fact is doing is wooing Orlando for herself. Paradoxes, ambiguities and absurdities abound. But the scene is far from being simply a farce. The undercurrent of real emotion is strong. We may be amused, but we should also be touched. After all, Rosalind is deeply, desperately in love (ll. 190–94):

> Oh coz, coz, coz, my pretty little coz, that thou didst know how many fathom deep I am in love! But it cannot be sounded: my affection hath an unknown bottom, like the Bay of Portugal.

It is such feeling as this that sustains Rosalind. As we watch this scene, we should be aware of how such rapture and slapstick lie side by side.

We should also notice how the moods in this scene change with breathtaking speed. We move from Rosalind's teasing of Orlando for being late to the suggestion (conveyed here, as in Act III, Scene iii, ll. 44–58, through the imagery of horns) that a woman can be unfaithful, and on to the teasing flirtatiousness of a kiss. Orlando, ever ready to run to extremes, says he would die without Rosalind. She knows that this is another of the exaggerated statements that lovers are prone to make. Her speech beginning at line 85 (which is full of classical references which you must be sure to look up and learn) is both practical, melancholy and sad. It is also full of wisdom. Rosalind is perfectly aware that no man has ever really died because of love. Then, suddenly, Rosalind's mood convincingly changes to 'a more coming-on disposition'. We have seen such quick and lively changes of mood in her before. Where? Rosalind is now both witty and serious. In such a mood she suggests a mock marriage. Celia is drawn in to play her part, but again the mood quickly changes. Rosalind doubts that Orlando will behave so charmingly as he does now when he is married. She tells him that his Rosalind will watch over him fiercely. And, once more, there is the suggestion that marriages are frail, that love does not last, that women must work hard to protect such relationships. As always in *As You Like It*, a subtle variety of moods is presented to us.

Then, quite suddenly, the supposedly love-sick Orlando remembers his obligation. He must leave his Rosalind for a couple of hours. He has to 'attend the Duke at dinner'. Although he promises to return, it is at this point that we must ask ourselves again which of the two is more deeply in love: Orlando, who, despite all his protestations, remembers his duty and leaves, or Rosalind, who tells him desperately that he must not dare to be late in coming back to her? We should also ask ourselves who has really done the wooing here: the young writer of poor love poetry, or the young girl dressed up as a boy?

The whole scene has affected Celia deeply and she rounds on Rosalind, telling her that she has behaved badly. Celia would prefer a woman to be much more demure. Rosalind is so deeply in love, however, that, as she tells Celia, she has thrown such proprieties to the wind.

ACT IV SCENE ii

This scene, which is very brief, is essentially an interlude to refresh us between the complicated passion we have just seen and the interview between Rosalind and Silvius which is to follow. Again, it is important to imagine its effect on the stage. Jaques and the Lords have been hunting. (Hunts were often, and understandably, used as symbols of a lover pursuing a beloved, and you may like to think that this scene comments on what we have just been watching.) The men sing a song – one of the many in the play – and so divert us before the next scene.

ACT IV SCENE iii

It seems that Orlando is late again. This calls forth some sharp comments from Celia, but the real – and highly melodramatic – reason for Orlando's delay will only become apparent later in the scene (ll. 99–157). Meanwhile, Silvius enters with Phebe's letter. He is clearly awed by the signs of wrath which the woman displayed when she wrote.

Rosalind too is somewhat surprised by the tone of the letter. Phebe has returned her taunts, and in such measure that Rosalind believes that Silvius himself must have written it. As she later says, 'This is a man's invention, and his hand'. Silvius swears his innocence. Rosalind continues to depict Phebe as a harsh, ugly and unfeminine person. The style of her letter is like a man's when he challenges another to a duel (ll. 32–3). Rosalind offers to read the letter aloud, but Silvius declares that he has heard too much of Phebe's shrill tongue. Nevertheless, as she reads the letter (which is in verse), Silvius is enraptured by its contents. Once again we see him as a foolish and completely doting lover. Phebe declares that Ganymede's eyes and anger have kindled her hopeless love. Ganymede must let her know, through Silvius, whether he will accept her love or dismiss her and leave her to die. Silvius is enraptured by the mere sound of Phebe's words, whereupon Celia pities him. Rosalind, on the other hand, though she is fully capable of extremes of love, is nonetheless a realist. She thinks that Silvius is absurd for allowing himself to be so dominated by a shrew such as Phebe. She tells him so, too. She adds 'that if she love me, I charge her to love thee'. In this way, at the close of the play, Rosalind will solve all these lovers' problems.

Oliver enters. The last we saw of him (in Act III, Scene i) was as a frightened courtier charged with seeking out his brother. But Oliver is now a changed man. He asks the disguised Celia and Rosalind for directions to a sheepcote. Celia gives them to him, and, as Oliver listens, so he begins to realize that he is talking to the couple for whom he is looking (ll. 84–90). They confess to being the people he is seeking and Oliver then presents his brother's compliments and mentions a 'bloody napkin' that Orlando has charged him to present to a youth whom he calls his Rosalind. Rosalind, of course, is immediately alarmed. Oliver offers to tell his story and so explains the situation.

The story that follows (ll. 99–157) is melodramatic and highly improbable. As such, it is wholly appropriate to the pastoral convention (see pp. 33, 84–7). Orlando has left Rosalind chewing 'the food of sweet and bitter fancy' – in other words, Orlando was lost in thoughts of love. Chancing to cast his eye aside as he walked along, Orlando noticed a poor and ragged man asleep under an ancient oak. A snake had wreathed itself about the man's neck. Seeing Orlando, the snake slunk away just as it was about to strike. A lioness was watching from the bushes, waiting for the man to stir. (It is part of the lion's royal nature, Oliver declares, that it scorns to attack anything that seems dead.) Orlando went over to the sleeping man and found him to be none other than his elder brother. We in the audience, of course, know this brother to be the man who is now speaking. However, neither Rosalind nor Celia realizes this as yet. Indeed, Celia comments (ll. 122–4) that she has heard Orlando tell how cruel and unnatural his brother is. Oliver agrees. Rosalind, naturally, is keen for him to tell the rest of his story. She wants to know about the bloody napkin. What has happened to Orlando? Did he leave his brother to fall prey to the lioness? Oliver tells her that he tried to do so twice. However, Orlando's kindness was finally stronger than his feeling of revenge and, in the end, he fought the lioness, 'who quickly fell before him'. (We are again reminded of Orlando's strength.) Of course, the noise of the fight woke the sleeping Oliver, who, by saying 'from miserable slumber *I* awaked', immediately reveals who he is.

Celia now asks a pointed question (l. 135):

> *Was't you that did so oft contrive to kill him?*

Oliver's cruel past comes to the fore. He confesses the truth of his previous plotting against Orlando, but – more importantly – tells how he has changed since his 'conversion'.

Rosalind is still concerned by the story of the 'bloody napkin'. Oliver declares that he will come to that in a moment and continues with his story. He tells how each of the brothers cheerfully recounted what had happened to him. Orlando then brought Oliver to the exiled Duke, who dressed him, entertained him and committed him to his brother's love. Orlando then led Oliver to his cave, and, fainting, showed him the wounds he had received in the fight with the lioness. As he fainted, Orlando – in true lover's fashion – called out for his Rosalind. Oliver bound up his brother's wounds, and, when Orlando had recovered, came to find Rosalind and present her with the 'bloody napkin', as he was asked to do. Rosalind sees the napkin and faints.

Celia tries to revive her. Oliver believes that 'he' (Rosalind is still disguised as Ganymede) has fainted at the sight of blood. Celia knows there is far more to it than this, but loyally preserves the disguise. Rosalind comes to. Oliver can scarcely believe that this Ganymede is indeed a man. He lacks, as he says, a man's heart. Rosalind agrees and tries to suggest that she only pretended to faint. Oliver clearly does not wholly believe her. He and Celia then bear the weak Rosalind away.

ACT V SCENE i

The last act opens with Touchstone and Audrey. Audrey is highly impatient at the delay in their marriage. Touchstone, meanwhile, realizes that he has a rival for her affection – or at least, for her hand in marriage. For her part, Audrey maintains that this man – his name is William – 'hath no interest in me in the world'.

William now enters. We should certainly think of him as the simplest type of 'stage countryman'. Notice how Touchstone lavishes his verbal trickery on him while William replies in the simplest phrases. On stage, the comic effect of this can be considerable.

For all that William confesses to love Audrey (l. 36), he makes no attempt whatever to win her back from Touchstone. Indeed, the clown's witty conversation is quite beyond William's intellectual reach. In his speech (ll. 45–56) Touchstone delights in finding pompous ways of telling William to leave and then rephrasing what he says in far more simple terms. Touchstone tells William to leave Audrey alone or else he will be forced to kill him. For her part, Audrey also asks William to go. The simple young man shuffles away without any protest. So much for him as a lover.

Corin enters to summon Touchstone to Rosalind and Celia.

ACT V SCENE ii

The newly reconciled Orlando and Oliver are talking together. It soon emerges that Oliver has fallen suddenly and desperately in love with Aliena – that is, Celia. He vows that he will give Orlando all their father's property and, with Celia, 'here live and die a shepherd'. Not only has Oliver been converted to good, he has also been wholly converted to the pastoral way of life.

Orlando agrees to the wedding and prepares to invite the Duke and his followers to it. Rosalind enters as Oliver leaves. Notice how his parting line (l. 18) shows that he is almost certainly aware that Ganymede is really a woman.

Left alone, the two lovers talk. Rosalind is grieved by Orlando's wound, and Orlando declares that he has really been wounded 'with the eyes of a lady'. Rosalind then reveals how deeply Celia and Oliver are in love. Orlando declares that 'they shall be married tomorrow', but this thought reminds him bitterly of how he is without the woman he loves. Rosalind – still, of course, dressed as Ganymede – asks if she can no longer serve in her place, and Orlando replies that she cannot (l. 48): 'I can live no longer by thinking'.

Rosalind then prepares for the final unravelling of the plot in which she will solve all the lovers' problems. She tells a highly improbable story. She declares that ever since she was three she has known a powerful magician whose tricks she has learned. She then says that tomorrow, when Oliver marries Celia, Orlando will marry his Rosalind. The implication is that Rosalind will be brought to Orlando by magic. In fact, as the audience and Rosalind well know, tomorrow will be the time when Rosalind reveals herself for the woman she really is. Orlando can barely believe his luck. Rosalind tells him (ll. 68–70) to

put you in your best array, bid your friends; for if you will be married tomorrow, you shall; and to Rosalind, if you will.

Silvius and Phebe enter. Phebe is angry that Rosalind has made the contents of her letter known to Silvius. Rosalind is indifferent to her and tells Phebe once again to be more fond of Silvius. Phebe orders Silvius to say what it is to be a lover. 'It is to be all made of sighs and tears,' he declares. His feelings find an echo in Phebe and Orlando. Rosalind, meanwhile, declares that she has such emotions 'for no woman'. Her heart, of course, as we know, is entirely Orlando's. On stage, the passage is delightfully ridiculous. However, Rosalind compares it to 'the howling of Irish wolves against the moon'. Having thus silenced them all, she then announces that she will bring their affairs to a happy conclusion. She will help Silvius if she can, declares she would love Phebe if she could, and will marry her 'if ever I marry woman'. She will also 'satisfy' Orlando, help Silvius to marry Phebe, and Orlando to marry Rosalind. All the lovers promise to meet her, and their meeting will, of course, provide the final happy ending to the play. Rosalind then departs.

ACT V SCENE iii

This scene is an interlude before the last great scene of the play. To effect the break, Shakespeare brings two of Duke Senior's pages on stage to sing the beautiful song 'It was a lover and his lass'. The country charm of the lyric, the invocation of spring and – on stage – the effect of the music are all delightful. We are reminded once again that we are in the pastoral world of love, poetry and music. And besides, as Touchstone says at the start of the scene (ll. 1–2):

Tomorrow is the joyful day, Audrey. Tomorrow we will be married.

ACT V SCENE iv

The last scene of the play is full of revelation and reconciliation. It is the perfect happy ending, saved from being too sentimental by the presence of Jaques.

The Duke asks Orlando if he really trusts Ganymede to do all that he has promised. Orlando hopes that he will but is unsure. Rosalind, still in her disguise, then enters. She asks the Duke (who, of course, is her father but still does not recognize her) if he will give Rosalind to Orlando if Rosalind can be produced. The Duke readily agrees. She then asks Orlando if he will accept Rosalind. He, too, readily agrees. Rosalind then asks Phebe if she will marry Ganymede if Ganymede so wishes. Phebe readily agrees to this. But, Rosalind says, if Phebe refuses to marry Ganymede (which seems at this stage highly unlikely), she will have to agree to marry Silvius. Phebe accepts these conditions. Needless to say, Silvius has no doubts about accepting Phebe. Having got all the parties to agree to these terms, the disguised Rosalind then leaves, going off to prepare a way 'to make these doubts all even'.

No sooner has she gone than Duke Senior begins to see how Ganymede resembles his daughter. Orlando declares that from the start he had wondered if 'he' were her brother. He adds, however, that 'this boy is forest-born'. For the moment, the disguise must remain intact.

Jaques announces the arrival of Touchstone and Audrey, introducing the former as 'the motley-minded gentleman that I have so often met in the forest'. He adds that Touchstone is a courtier. Touchstone boasts that this is indeed true and then declares his desire to marry Audrey. Touchstone's witty comments are clearly appreciated and, sensing this, he elaborates on his supposed experience of duelling. His analysis of this and of 'a lie seven times removed' is an amusing satire of courtly manners, a show-piece of wit which a good stage clown can make very humorous indeed. And it is just this mixture of foolery and wisdom that so appeals to Jaques (ll. 101–2).

Again, what follows is wholly designed for the stage, and in the theatre is a beautiful and even solemn moment. A masquer (actor) dressed as the god of marriage, Hymen, enters with Rosalind and Celia, who are now no longer in disguise. Hymen – who should be beautiful to behold – then sings a song of love and reconciliation. He presents Rosalind to her father and asks him, in turn, to offer Rosalind in marriage to Orlando. When the song is over, Rosalind offers herself to both of them: her father first, and then her future husband. Both rapturously accept her. Only Phebe is cheated, and her disappointment must inevitably make us smile. As so often in the play, two apparently contradictory moods are brought together. Rosalind answers her father and her lover in turn. She then addresses the woman who has been mistakenly pursuing her.

Hymen settles the 'confusion'. He joins together Orlando and Rosalind, Oliver and Celia, Phebe and Silvius, Touchstone and Audrey. Four marriages are made and the ceremony concludes with a song. Duke Senior welcomes Rosalind and Celia, Phebe welcomes Silvius. Happiness has at last been found.

But this is not quite all. Right at the very start of the play Orlando told us of an elder brother called Jaques. Now we meet him. He enters to tell us of yet another surprising but happy turn of events. Duke Frederick, hearing how 'men of great worth' have been flocking to the side of Duke Senior, whose lands he had usurped, raised an army and was about to come and put Duke Senior to death. But, like Oliver, he too has been through a conversion. At the edge of the forest he met 'an old religious man', who persuaded him to give up evil worldly ends, restore his stolen crown to his brother, return their lands to the exiled lords and lead a hermit's virtuous life.

The Duke welcomes the news, declaring that Oliver now has his lands restored to him (they were seized in Act III, Scene i). Orlando, of course, by his marriage to Rosalind, has become the heir to the dukedom. The penniless young man of the start of the play now has a beautiful wife and great prospects. However, the newly restored Duke Senior declares that they will not return to the court immediately, but rather will celebrate with 'rustic revelry'.

'The melancholy Jaques' interposes. He intends to follow Duke Frederick into his 'religious' life away from 'the pompous court'. Jaques will not be dissuaded from this. Rather, he congratulates Duke Senior on the reverse in his fortunes, and tells Orlando that he deserves his happiness, Oliver his lands and Silvius his love. As for Touchstone and Audrey, Jaques is too realistic not to see that their marriage is unlikely to last. They will be quarrelling after two months. Perhaps he is right. What he says here both confirms the happy ending and stops it from being too perfect. When he has left, the Duke bids all the rest join him. Only Rosalind is left. She speaks the epilogue. She steps out of character, breaks the dramatic illusion, and wittily urges the audience to applaud the play that they have been watching.

Characters

ROSALIND

Rosalind is one of the most delightful of Shakespeare's heroines. She is witty, resilient and capable of deep affection. It is Rosalind who, in her various moods, absorbs much of our interest during the course of the play. Finally, it is she who helps to bring the comedy to its happy conclusion.

We hear about her before we actually meet her. Oliver asks the wrestler, Charles, if Rosalind has followed her banished father into exile. At once it is made clear that Rosalind is an aristocrat – an almost essential qualification for a heroine of pastoral (see pp. 33, 84–7). Charles's reply, however, tells us more about Rosalind's personal characteristics. It is these that will delight and move us during the course of *As You Like It*. Charles tells Oliver that rather than go with her father into the Forest of Arden, Rosalind has elected to stay close by her friend Celia, who is, we learn, the daughter of the usurping Duke. Celia is thus Rosalind's cousin. The great affection between the two girls is made clear, as is the fact that Rosalind's delightful character attracts all who meet her. At this stage, even the usurping Duke Frederick holds her in high regard. Indeed, he is as fond of Rosalind as he is of his own daughter. His feelings, of course, will suddenly and violently change.

Nonetheless, when we first meet Rosalind, in Act I, Scene ii, the bright, attractive girl we have been led to expect is not at first evident. Rosalind is depressed. She is suffering from that melancholy or lack of spirits that makes up an important part of *As You Like It* and which Shakespeare shows in much of its variety. Rosalind's sadness is, naturally, the result of thinking about what has happened to her father. She can forget neither him nor what has happened. Celia tries to comfort her (and thus makes clear again the great friendship that Rosalind inspires in others), but it is as much Rosalind's natural resilience, her refusal to give in to sad thoughts, that cause her mood to change. Like a sudden burst of sunshine, Rosalind declares that from henceforth she will be more cheerful and 'devise sports'. She thinks immediately of falling in love. Celia, the more reserved of the two girls, is slightly abashed by this, and the exchange of wit that follows, the intricate and amusing play with words that is another characteristic of *As You Like It*, shows how agile a mind Rosalind has. This is an important part of her character.

Then Touchstone enters, and the conversation that follows shows once more the alert but kindly delight in life that Rosalind so often reveals. Again, her reaction to the somewhat absurd figure of Le Beau reveals her wit, but when she agrees with Touchstone that the cruel wrestling bout that the courtier describes is hardly fit entertainment for ladies, we are reminded once more that Rosalind, for all her wit and irony, has delicate feelings. It is this more serious side of her nature that we will soon be made aware of. The heroine is about to meet the hero of the play. Rosalind is about to fall in love.

At the request of Duke Frederick, Rosalind and Celia try to dissuade Orlando from entering the wrestling match. However, despite their solicitude, he will not be deflected from his purpose. Orlando is at once courteous and movingly honest in what he says. Life, he suggests, holds nothing for him. If he is killed in a wrestling match, then so be it.

Rosalind is deeply moved by Orlando. His combination of breeding and pathos, youth, bravery and hopelessness, rouses her feelings and, of course, reminds her of her own sad state. As she wishes on Orlando 'the little strength that I have', so we sense the first stirrings of her love for him. We should note that the words of the play do not at this moment suggest that Orlando returns her feelings, but a full stage production will almost certainly make this clear. We may perhaps guess that it is just this new love – unspoken as yet – that gives Orlando the will to win. Certainly, the wrestling match is a most important stage in the affair between him and Rosalind, and to realize its full impact we have again to imagine the play in production. The fight should be an exciting one. We must feel Rosalind's mounting concern for the fate of the young man of whom she has started to grow fond. After all, we have learned from Le Beau that to wrestle with Charles can be a matter of life and death. As Rosalind calls out her encouragement, we should feel her excitement and concern, her relief and sense of triumph as Charles is thrown.

Duke Frederick is furious when he learns of Orlando's parentage: Orlando's father, Sir Rowland de Boys, was his enemy. However, the dead man was a friend of Rosalind's father, and this is another bond between the two young people. When the girls go over to congratulate Orlando, Rosalind presents him with a gold chain. This is a quiet but touching declaration of her feelings. She immediately turns to go. It is when she leaves that Orlando is for the first time fully aware of the power this girl has over him. He too has fallen deeply and suddenly in love. Rosalind turns to him. She feels no need for pride or haughtiness. This ability to give herself to the man she loves is important: it is what underlies the rest of her conduct in the play.

Celia then urges her away, and when we next see the girls (Act I, Scene iii), Rosalind is in her melancholy mood once more. This time, however, her melancholy is caused by love. We have seen that the pastoral convention requires sudden and violent turns of fortune (for a further discussion see pp. 33 and 84–7). At this moment Duke Frederick enters and, as we have been warned, reveals his impulsive hatred for Rosalind and banishes her from the court. Rosalind pleads her own case eloquently and with dignity. Duke Frederick, however, will not be moved. He calls Celia a fool for loving the girl and then repeats his sentence of banishment.

Rosalind's resilience and love of life that we have noted before now come to the surface. At first she is utterly despondent at the sentence imposed on her, but as Celia shows her great love for her and suggests that they both run away to the Forest of Arden, so Rosalind's imagination is kindled. She accepts Celia's plan and develops it so that it becomes almost her own invention. She suggests that she dress herself in 'all points like a man', assume the name Ganymede and that she and Celia take Touchstone with them on their journey. This rapid, delightful change from despondency to resilient liveliness is a feature of Rosalind and is partly what makes her so endearing a character.

But for all her father's praise of the country life (Act II, Scene i), the pastoral existence is not a simple delight. When we meet the three travellers – Rosalind, Celia and Touchstone – they are tired, hungry and very depressed. The Forest of Arden is not at first all that it promised to be. Nonetheless, it is a place of comedy. Corin enters with Silvius, a young shepherd who is hopelessly and absurdly in love with Phebe. We are shown the ridiculous and painful sides of love simultaneously: we may laugh at Silvius, but when Rosalind declares that his feelings remind her of her own for Orlando, we are reminded also that love can be a painful and serious business.

Celia, more down-to-earth, suggests that they all find something to eat. She bids Touchstone ask Corin for food. The clown does so with the ridiculous pomposity of a courtier advising a simple countryman. We laugh, but Rosalind's interventions show again the natural friendliness she has towards all people. She asks Corin simply and directly for food, rest and shelter. Corin's reply shows us that, as we already know, the country life is far from ideal. Corin has a cruel master and barely enough food for himself. Besides, the farm on which he works is up for sale. Rosalind's quick mind at once sees a possibility here. The girls have brought some of their gold and jewellery with them: should they not use these to buy the farm? Celia agrees that this would be a fine idea. Corin, of course, is delighted by this sudden change in his prospects, and we in the audience guess both that the farm will be bought and that the disguised Rosalind and Celia will set up as shepherds in the true pastoral tradition.

We do not meet Rosalind again until Act II, Scene iv. Instead, we return to the exiled courtiers and encounter Orlando and hear of Jaques, after we have seen Duke Frederick issuing an order for Oliver to seek out his brother. This interval not only allows Shakespeare to introduce us to some important characters and develop his plot, but also suggests the passing of time, during which the pastoral idyll of Rosalind and Celia has become an established way of life for them.

We know that love is a major preoccupation of the pastoral world, and it is with love in our minds that we are reintroduced to Rosalind. By the beginning of Act III, Scene ii, Orlando has returned to thoughts of her and – in true lover's fashion – has become a poet. We see him nailing his verses to a tree, something which, we will learn, it is his habit to do. We should note here that the concerned and brave young man of the earlier scenes has been replaced by a more light-hearted, more comic character. In the heat of his passion, Orlando is close to Silvius. Both young men show the absurdities, delights and pains of extreme love.

Touchstone (not without some justification) considers Orlando to be a very poor poet and provides an instant and rather shrewd parody of the verses that Rosalind has found. When Celia enters, reading yet more of Orlando's poetry, even Rosalind is forced to admit that the verses are a 'tedious homily of love'. In other words, Orlando's poetry brings together many of the clichés of contemporary love-verse. This is yet another way in which Shakespeare satirizes the pastoral convention.

Celia wonders if Rosalind has not guessed who wrote these verses in her praise. Rosalind swears she has not. Celia gently teases her into remembering Orlando and, as she does so, Rosalind's words beautifully convey the excitement, the breathless welcoming of love. Though she is disguised as Ganymede, she declares her feelings to be a woman's through and through. As the truth dawns on her that Orlando is indeed the poet who is praising her, so the love that she has felt ever since she met him at the wrestling match begins to grow. Rosalind declares with horror (III, ii, 212–13):

Alas the day, what shall I do with my doublet and hose.

It is just this absurd situation – that, though dressed as a boy, she is in fact a woman desperately in love with a young man – which will provide the comedy in the following scenes.

It is Rosalind's characteristics of wit and a sense of fun that now come to the fore. As Orlando enters talking to Jaques, she feels he is a hunter come 'to kill my heart'. When Jaques leaves, she determines to speak to Orlando 'like a saucy lackey'. Rosalind will exploit her disguise rather than regret that she is forced to wear it. Orlando will think she is a boy and she will 'play the knave with him'.

What follows is a beautiful, subtle, but difficult scene. The language is complex and fast-moving, and you must use the notes in your edition to make sure you fully understand it. Only then will you be able to appreciate the true comedy and the underlying seriousness. What, in fact, is happening? Rosalind, disguised as a boy, is teasing the man she loves (and who loves her) by saying that he has none of the marks of a true lover about him. She wins his interest through her wit and, having convinced Orlando that she is a 'pretty youth', furthers the deception by telling him that she is a native of the forest and lives there with her sister. Orlando recognizes that her voice is an educated one and, on top of the already delightfully absurd situation, Rosalind fabricates a story of having been brought up by 'an old religious uncle'. He has lectured against love, and Rosalind (in her disguise as Ganymede, of course) declares that she could use what her uncle has taught her to cure the young lover who is disfiguring the forest trees by carving the name 'Rosalind' on their barks and pinning his poems to them. Orlando confesses to his authorship of the poems and admits his desperate passion. Rosalind's wit, insight and sense of fun are now fully alerted. She again states that Orlando bears none of the signs of a true lover, but says that she could 'cure' Orlando's love, which she interprets as a form of lunacy: 'I profess curing it by counsel'. She suggests an absurd but wholly delightful course of treatment. Orlando must pretend that Ganymede is his Rosalind. She will then prove so contrary in her moods that Orlando will give up love altogether. The irony here is delightfully complex. Rosalind, dressed as a boy, is both courting and testing her lover by having him believe in her disguise and then pretending that she really is his Rosalind. She will 'cure' him of his love while in fact courting him. Orlando agrees to this complex deception 'with all my heart'.

But Orlando is late for their first meeting. The fourth scene of Act III opens with Rosalind's resulting unhappiness. 'His very hair is of the dissembling colour,' she says in her wretchedness. Celia too suggests that Orlando is not a true lover. The depth of Rosalind's feelings for him is nonetheless made clear. The two girls are then interrupted by the arrival of Corin, who leads them to where Silvius and Phebe are having a lovers' quarrel. This is not only amusing, but also, as Rosalind becomes involved, it makes us aware of how she is required to play some part in other people's affairs of the heart. Shakespeare has constructed this play to show Rosalind in a wide variety of roles. Here we see her – still disguised as Ganymede – as the arbiter between the two country lovers. Notice how, with the help of her disguise, she is tart, forthright and vigorous in what she says. She is completely frank with Phebe, and while this prevents Rosalind herself from appearing as merely the unhappy lover that we saw earlier and so diversifies our reaction to her, it is just this harshness in her tone that so attracts Phebe. The country girl falls in love with the disguised Rosalind, and from this all manner of complications ensue. Shakespeare thus succeeds in showing another and perhaps unexpected side of her character, while also developing his plot.

This witty resilience in Rosalind's character serves her well in her meeting with Jaques (Act IV, Scene i), and she uses it again to chide Orlando when he does finally turn up to their meeting. You should notice how, in this delicate and witty encounter, Rosalind's moods vary from the tone of the 'saucy lackey' through excited love to delicate but wise melancholy (ll. 85–98). She is as 'changeable' as, in Act III, Scene ii, ll. 391–402, she promised Ganymede would be. Celia is shocked at her behaviour and declares that Rosalind has 'simply misused our sex'. But Rosalind is not to be criticized in this way. She is a young woman frankly and fully in love, a fact she rapturously announces (ll. 190–93):

> Oh coz, coz, coz, my pretty little coz, that thou didst know how many fathom deep I am in love! But it cannot be sounded: my affection hath an unknown bottom, like the Bay of Portugal.

The third scene of Act IV shows us once again the quick changes of mood that Shakespeare has created for his heroine. We last saw her head over heels with the excitement of love. Now she is despondent. Once again Orlando has failed to turn up for their date. Just as before (Act III, Scene v) this mood was interrupted by the mention of Silvius and Phebe, so now Silvius enters to present the disguised Rosalind with Phebe's 'chiding' letter. Rosalind is angered by its tone, but, in her concluding speech to Silvius (ll. 67–70), we hear again that shrewd but kindly consideration, that concern for others, which is so important a part of her character.

The entry of Oliver returns us from the delightful world of shepherds in love to that other aspect of pastoral we have noted – sudden and dramatic turns in events. Oliver recounts the story of how Orlando has saved him from wild animals, overcome his own desire for revenge, forgiven his brother and become reconciled with him. Our opinion of Orlando reverts to that which we formed of him at the start of the play: no longer is he just the mildly absurd lover, he is the strong, well-bred young man with whom Rosalind at first fell in love. And the more that Oliver's speeches reinforce this impression, the more the still-disguised Rosalind's feminine feelings assert themselves. She listens to Oliver's story with baited breath and mounting excitement. Finally, as she hears of Orlando's wounds, she faints and, when she recovers, only with difficulty maintains her disguise as a man. And indeed, the time is now approaching when she will have to reveal herself for who she really is.

When she meets Orlando again (Act V, Scene ii), it is to discuss the wedding of Celia to Orlando's brother Oliver. For Orlando, the forthcoming wedding will cause 'the height of heart-heaviness'. Rosalind in her disguise as Ganymede will no longer suffice him. His melancholy suggests the true depths of his real affection. Rosalind is moved, and with the delight in the highly unlikely, which, as we have seen, is a part of the pastoral convention, she invents a way of solving the problem. She declares she 'can do strange things'. She is, she says, the pupil of a magician. She can work magic. As a result, 'If you do love Rosalind so near the heart as your gesture cries it out, when your brother marries Aliena, shall you marry her.' Orlando can barely believe her, of course, but he is reassured by the time that Phebe and Silvius enter. A delightfully comic dialogue takes place, with Silvius sighing for Phebe, and Rosalind declaring she sighs 'for no woman'. The dialogue sounds, as Rosalind says, 'like the howling of Irish wolves against the moon'. She brings it to a close by announcing that she will solve the problems of all of them. She will help Silvius, for when she reveals herself as Rosalind, it will be impossible for Phebe to marry her, and so the country girl will have to honour her promise to marry Silvius if she rejects Ganymede. Phebe will then finally be married, as will Orlando. The comedy will be brought to a happy conclusion.

This is the subject of the last scene. Rosalind, in her disguise as Ganymede for the last time, enters to ask her father the Duke to accept his daughter when she appears and the others to be true to the promises they have sworn. She and Celia then leave. When they return (l. 105) it is, as the stage directions say, 'as themselves'. But although Rosalind and Celia are no longer in disguise, this does not mean we have yet returned to the real world. Indeed, far from it. The girls enter with 'a masquer representing Hymen'. Hymen is the God of Marriage, and he is accompanied by music. On stage, the effect is serene, almost unearthly, and just as the music is harmonious, so harmony is restored to the characters. Married love takes the place of confusion. Rosalind's unravelling of the comic complications of the plot, when she reveals herself to her father and plights herself to Orlando, shows her in her final role as a bringer of peace and love, a mood developed in Hymen's words and final song. Only Jaques adds that taste of bitterness which prevents the conclusion from becoming too sentimental.

And finally Shakespeare breaks the dramatic illusion he has created. As the actors leave the stage, Rosalind is left alone. At the end of the complicated plot we have been watching, Rosalind threw off her disguise as a boy to become Orlando's wife. Now, for the audience, the actor throws off his disguise as the girl Rosalind and begs their applause.

Throughout the highly complex developments of the plot of *As You Like It*, Shakespeare manages to show Rosalind in a wide variety of moods. She is, above all, a radiantly healthy and extrovert young girl, intelligent, witty and capable of deep feeling. She can both attract and give affection. Her character is given further depth by occasional bouts of melancholy. All the many different aspects of her nature, her energy, sense of humour and realism, compel our interest and affection.

ORLANDO

Orlando is the hero of the play. He introduces it and immediately arouses our sympathy. He tells us that he is the youngest son of Sir Rowland de Boys, that he has been left a very small amount of money by his father, and that his elder brother, Oliver, treats him with great cruelty. From the start it is clear that Orlando is an attractive character, intelligent, well bred and in a desperate situation. It appears that he has almost no friends in the world except old Adam, to whom he describes his plight as an impoverished younger son with no hopes.

One of the aspects of Orlando's personality that is particularly attractive is his refusal to tolerate the life that he is living. It is important to recognize that Orlando is strong both in mind and in body. Later, when we see him in the Forest of Arden, he may seem rather absurd. This is because Shakespeare is showing the excesses of love. Both the opening scene and his later fights with the wrestler Charles and the lion show us that Orlando is very far from being a weak and foppish young man. Right at the start he challenges his brother, putting his case strongly and thus winning our sympathy. Later, when he comes to the wrestling match, he presents himself in an attractive light again – indeed, his dignified description of his sad life endears him to Rosalind. This is the beginning of the love-affair between them. It is most important that we visualize the fight as we read the play. Here, above all, we see Orlando's physical strength. He has impressed us as an active, intelligent and sympathetic character, and now we see that he can stand up for himself against the strongest man in the country. Orlando wins the fights, of course, and, in so doing, he wins Rosalind's love as well.

It is important to recognize that in addition to the qualities we have already described, Orlando is a young man of delicate feelings. Far from exulting in his victory over the wrestler Charles (and, though he does not realize this, thereby saving himself from his brother Oliver's evil plot to destroy him), Orlando is aware that he has been 'thrown' by Rosalind's beauty. He is now a young man ardently in love. These new emotions are a joyful confusion to him.

However, the evil world in which Orlando lives still threatens him. He returns home after the wrestling match only to discover that Oliver will go to any lengths to be rid of him. As old Adam tells him, his brother is even prepared to burn him to death. Orlando must flee at all costs. But Orlando has no friends and no money. In a most touching scene, old Adam offers both his friendship and his lifetime's savings to this worthy young man, the true and honourable heir of Sir Rowland de Boys. It is a measure of Orlando's delicacy that he accepts this touching offer with deep gratitude. He does not take advantage of old Adam; rather, he welcomes the old retainer's kindness and together they go off to seek their fortunes.

Eventually, of course, they arrive in the Forest of Arden. We have learned from the exiled Duke that the forest can be a delightful place of escape. We also learn that it can be harsh and even cruel. When we next see Orlando and Adam (Act II, Scene vi), the utterly faithful old man is exhausted. Orlando again earns our sympathy and respect by refusing to let him die and, instead, going off to search for food once he is sure that the old man is safe. Orlando's bravery impresses us once again when he bursts in on Duke Senior's feast and demands food. The Duke recognizes Orlando's courtesy and bids him join them, but Orlando refuses to do so until he has brought Adam to the feast. While he is fetching the old man, Jaques delivers his famous speech on 'The

Seven Ages of Man' – a cynical and bitter view of human life. It is a view that we reject when we see the brave and loyal Orlando carrying his exhausted servant in.

Once established in the Forest of Arden, we see a wholly different side to Orlando's character. He fell in love with Rosalind at the wrestling match and now that love burgeons into something amusing and excessive. Obsessed by his passion in a way that reminds us of the foolish young Silvius, Orlando rushes round the forest pinning his rather bad love-poems to every tree. It is when he is in this state that he again encounters Rosalind, who, of course, is now disguised as Ganymede.

The scenes between these two lovers that follow are difficult for two reasons. Firstly, their language is witty and intricate; to understand it we must use the notes in our edition carefully. Secondly, if we are only reading the play, we have to imagine the complex situation in which Rosalind, the woman who loves Orlando, is disguised as a boy; while Orlando, the man who loves Rosalind, is voluntarily undergoing a cure for the 'madness' of love by submitting to the teaching of Ganymede. Rosalind is simultaneously testing Orlando's true feelings, teasing him and amusing us. Orlando has become the very model of the foolish lover, though his feelings are true ones.

But the old Orlando, the brave and dignified young man we met at the start, has not disappeared. After he has failed for a second time to appear for a meeting with Rosalind, we learn the reason for his delay. He has found his evil brother in a state of mortal danger and has let his better feelings master him. He has saved Oliver from certain death at great danger to himself. Oliver, as we know, falls instantly and deeply in love with Celia. His love is returned. The prospect of their happiness makes Orlando deeply melancholy. However, the Rosalind with whom he has fallen in love is a passionately loyal and intelligent character. Through his complete trust in her – the sign of his true love – Orlando is eventually reunited with her. The sad hero that we saw at the start of the play has now completed the series of trials which test both his resilience and the depth of his love. As is right, at the end of the play he wins his bride.

JAQUES

Jaques is one of the most important characters in *As You Like It* and also one of the most difficult to understand. He is described in the play as 'the melancholy Jaques', and this helps us to appreciate what Shakespeare was trying to suggest through him.

You should note that Jaques contributes almost nothing in terms of the plot of the play. His role is to talk, to comment. He exists to provide a particular tone of cynical world-weariness, bitterness and criticism. His 'melancholy' stops the play from becoming too sentimental, but it is not an end in itself. Shakespeare shows us that Jaques's view of life is an affectation that has very real limits. *As You Like It* is a play about love, growth and trust. Jaques shows almost none of these characteristics. Rather, he is determined to satirize what he sees as a whole world of foolishness about him. What he does not realize is that many of the characters in the play see him as being distinctly foolish himself.

It is as a foolish and affected man that he is first described to us. He is depicted as being alone in the woods, 'moralizing' on the death of a deer. This provides the courtiers with much amusement. Nonetheless, if we read their words carefully, we will see that Jaques is perfectly well aware of the foolish escapism that Duke Senior and his friends are indulging in and of their delight in a pastoral world. Jaques sees that this has limitations. In Act II, Scene v, Jaques amusingly satirizes Amiens and the other courtiers, but in Act II, Scene vii, when he has met Touchstone, we see him in his true role: he wishes to be like Touchstone, a licensed fool who can be as abusive about people's follies as he wishes. He believes that only those who really are foolish will be offended by what he says. But if Jaques is setting himself up as the man who can see through human weakness, he is, nonetheless, nowhere near as virtuous as he might seem. As the Duke points out, Jaques has been 'a libertine' in his youth, a man who once practised all the follies and vices against which he now rails. However, Jaques's affectation of bitterness, his caustic wit and his ingenuity with words are all hugely entertaining. They rise to a climax in Act II, Scene vii, when, at l. 140, he has his great speech on 'The Seven Ages of Man'. This is a brilliant and deservedly famous speech. It is a masterpiece of cynical insight. Jaques sees mankind only in terms of caricature; it is absurd and worthy of being laughed at. Nonetheless, he is capable of vivid detail which enhances his power to destroy. But, as we have seen, none of the would-be destroyers – Oliver, Duke Frederick, Jaques himself – succeeds. Jaques may convince us here, but the entry of Orlando with old Adam in his arms obliterates Jaques's world-hating picture. Charity replaces scorn. From this point on, we may respect Jaques's ability to see through folly and expose it, but we also know that his view of life has severe limitations.

We are certainly amused when he mocks another affected man: Orlando, who is now playing the part of the smitten lover. Jaques's tart comments prepare us for the mild absurdities of behaviour that Orlando displays in his dialogue with Rosalind in Act III, Scene ii. At the beginning of Act IV we see Jaques in conversation with Rosalind, who is, of course, disguised as Ganymede. Jaques sees this as a golden opportunity to show off, but Rosalind is merely amused and is perfectly capable of standing her own ground.

Throughout the play, Jaques's tart comments on human folly have either been reported to us or been overheard by us. He glides through the play spying or being spied on and ridiculing absurdity. He has a view of life that we have called bitter and cynical, and he constantly tries to force on other characters in the play the idea that his view of the world is the only true and really valuable one. What he has to say is certainly powerful and often valid, and he does have great insight. He can see right through the relationship between Touchstone and Audrey, for example, and knows that this unlikely marriage will not last for more than two months. We can, perhaps, thus respect Jaques as a man of insight, but overall we cannot really accept his view of the world. The courtiers laugh at him, Orlando and Rosalind are no more than amused by him, Duke Senior can see right through him. In a play about human love Jaques can expose affectation and absurdity but, in the end, he has no place among the happy lovers and the court of the restored Duke. Love and harmony are shown to be more powerful than cynicism.

And yet we cannot help having some affection for Jaques. He is a wonderfully extreme, inventive and affected fool. We feel that there is true poetic justice when, with a few shrewd words to the united lovers, he leaves their company to join the newly converted Duke Frederick in his life as a hermit. Jaques's obsession with human folly – a folly that he does not recognize in himself – finally leads him to join a saddened group of men who have willingly placed themselves outside the confines of prosperous and harmonious love with which the play ends.

OLIVER

At the start of *As You Like It*, Oliver is the true 'stage villain'. His hatred for Orlando is excessively violent, deeply sinister and wholly irrational. It also fails to achieve its end – the destruction of Orlando. Although Oliver blackens his younger brother's character to the wrestler Charles in a wholly convincing way, what Oliver does not realize is that Orlando's strengths are not just those of youth and goodness which attract everyone he meets. Orlando is also physically strong, and in an exciting combat he throws the Duke's wrestler.

Duke Frederick is, like Oliver himself, something of a 'stage villain'. He is furious that Orlando has not only overthrown Charles but is also the son of Sir Rowland de Boys, a worthy figure who makes him feel deeply and uncomfortably ashamed of himself. Duke Frederick, with a passionate hatred of the good identical to that which Oliver shows to his brother, seizes Oliver's property and orders him to find Orlando or be exiled. Evil men, Shakespeare shows, destroy each other.

We do not see Oliver again until Act IV, Scene iii, and it is a very different man that we meet. He has been sent by his brother to tell Rosalind and Celia how he has been saved from certain death through Orlando's goodness and strength. As a result of Orlando's goodness, his inability to let his wicked brother die, Oliver has undergone a sudden and total conversion. Such things are characteristic of the pastoral convention (see pp. 33, 84–7).

Not only has Oliver seen the error of his ways, but now that he is a reformed man he is capable of love. He falls deeply for Celia, and his feelings are returned. Of course, it is all highly unlikely, but that is why it is so amusing. Nonetheless, Shakespeare manages to convince us that Oliver's conversion is genuine and, perhaps partly because we are happy to see Celia happily married, we feel that Oliver too has earned his place among the newly-weds at the end of the play.

CELIA

Shakespeare's presentation of Celia is particularly effective, for while she must serve through most of the play as a foil to Rosalind, she is nonetheless a character in her own right. Intensely loyal and loving, she is devoted to Rosalind's well-being, and this is made clear as soon as we see her in Act I, Scene ii. We admire the way in which she stands up to her own father when he has banished Rosalind. And also it is Celia's idea that both girls should run off to the Forest of Arden. Celia is thus both courageous and admirable, but she does not have the radiant love of life and glorious high spirits that make Rosalind so very attractive and so natural a leader. Celia is much more reserved; and, of course, throughout the greater part of the play she is not in love. This allows her to view the behaviour of the other lovers objectively. She points out to Rosalind what she considers to be the excesses of her cousin's behaviour and is critical of Orlando, albeit in a way that shows her abiding loyalty to Rosalind.

But Celia is far from being a dreary character: she is energetic, responsible, kindly. And, finally, she too has her place amongst the happy and newly wed characters. It is for Celia that the recently reformed Oliver falls, and it is clear that his feelings are returned. We are never shown Oliver and Celia alone on stage together. We are only told that they have suddenly fallen in love. We believe in the sincerity of this and are glad that these two can take their place amongst the happily reconciled young people at the close of the play.

TOUCHSTONE

Shakespeare frequently introduces a 'fool' into his plays. Sometimes they are bitter; sometimes, as with Touchstone, they are kindly men; but in all cases they are people who speak the truth. This aspect of Touchstone's character is suggested by his name: a 'touchstone', as we have seen (p. 27), was a means of testing the value of alloys of silver and gold. In the play Touchstone helps to show the purities and impurities of some of the characters he meets. Like all of Shakespeare's fools, Touchstone relishes words: puns, jokes and stories abound.

Perhaps this is shown at its most elaborate in Act V, Scene iv, where he gives a virtuoso display in his satire of the courtly life.

However, while Touchstone is a professional entertainer and remains such throughout the play, Shakespeare also presents a number of other aspects of his personality. For example, when we first meet him in the second scene, we are struck by his capacity for friendship and for the honest appraisal of what is going on about him. He is appalled by Le Beau's description of the old man and his three sons at the wrestling match. This immediately wins the audience's sympathy for Touchstone, and we feel that Rosalind and Celia, when they are obliged to flee the court, are in safe – if not altogether responsible – company.

Touchstone is pre-eminently a man of the court. Although he develops a strong liking for the countryside and its people, he cannot help feeling superior to all those he meets. His skill with language amusingly exposes the conventional slow-wittedness of country folk, and he runs rings round Corin, Audrey and William. And yet, as he does so, we strongly suspect that he is not in his true element.

Touchstone's love for Audrey is yet another way in which Shakespeare shows the delights and follies of pastoral love. The relationship between Touchstone and Audrey is more physical, less responsible and far less permanent than all the other affairs in the play, but it does have its own earthy poetry and provides an important tone to *As You Like It*. At the end of the play it is of course Jaques – the bitter, satirical and melancholy fool – who exposes Touchstone's affair with Audrey for what it is. However, whichever aspect of Touchstone's character Shakespeare is portraying, we cannot help but like him. He may be something of a rogue who considers himself superior to many of those about him, but his kindliness and loyalty to Rosalind and Celia ensure that he retains our sympathy and warmth for him.

AUDREY

Audrey is the simple, down-to-earth and probably rather voluptuous girl with whom Touchstone amuses himself while he is in the Forest of Arden. We have barely met her when Touchstone informs us he has agreed to marry her and has even lined up the vicar. Jaques, who has watched their whole conversation, steps in to prevent Touchstone from being 'married under a bush like a beggar', but it is important to note that the idea of 'not being well married' appeals to Touchstone. It suggests to him the possibility of giving Audrey up as lightly as he came by her.

Just as Touchstone does not really relish the idea of his relationship with Audrey being a long-term one, so in Act V, Scene i, Audrey can lightly give up William, her previous and rather stupid friend. By a nice paradox, she has chosen to marry a real 'fool' instead. While there is a sense of irresponsibility about the relationship between Touchstone and Audrey – a relationship which is probably based on little more than the pressing need to sleep with each other – Shakespeare is not cynical in his presentation of their affair. Act V, Scene iii shows Touchstone and Audrey together waiting to be married 'tomorrow'. Two pages enter and sing for them one of the loveliest of all Shakespeare's songs: 'It was a lover and his lass'. The charm of this song – and here again we must think of its effect on stage – gives the relationship between Touchstone and Audrey a very beautiful quality. The song captures the essence of happy-go-lucky country life which lies near the centre of the pastoral. And, of course, right at the end of the play Jaques's sour comment on Touchstone and Audrey's marriage, his belief that it is 'but for two months victualled', provides the slightly bitter note of realism which prevents the end of the play from being over-sentimental.

WILLIAM

As You Like It is set, as we have seen, in the pastoral world. Though Shakespeare makes us smile at many of his simple rustic characters, he usually presents them as having honest virtues or – by and large – good hearts. William, who has been Audrey's sometime lover, appears only in Act V, Scene i, and he is a cartoon picture of the simple, country yokel. Touchstone has great fun with this man who is barely capable of speaking words of more than one syllable, of understanding what Touchstone says or of striving to win back his girlfriend. He exists only to make us laugh.

SILVIUS

Silvius, a shepherd, is a delightful comic invention. Passionately and ridiculously in love, he is a character who helps to show the 'extremes' into which lovers can run. His delicacy and extreme ardour form a delightfully comic contrast to the harsh, down-to-earth Phebe, for whom he pines. He is entirely at Phebe's mercy. She, of course, plays the part of the cruel mistress, humiliating him and ordering him about, much to our amusement. Silvius is put in the ridiculous position of having to deliver his own mistress's love-letter to Rosalind while she is disguised as Ganymede. Rosalind appreciates that Silvius's feelings for Phebe are genuine, and it is part of Rosalind's attractive and level-headed generosity that she can solve Silvius's problems and finally bring about his marriage to the woman he loves.

PHEBE

Phebe is the plain country girl who enjoys playing the part of the cruel mistress. Shakespeare's presentation of her is comic and is one of the ways in which he makes us laugh at the pastoral life. We are first introduced to Phebe by seeing the effect she has on Silvius. She makes him run into 'many actions most ridiculous'. When we first meet her in Act III, Scene v, we are probably surprised that a plain, ordinary girl can rouse such feelings. We also see that Phebe has a shrewd eye for pretentiousness, as when she punctures the inflated poetic language of Silvius. But no sooner has she done so than she meets Rosalind disguised as Ganymede, falls head over heels in love herself and adopts the same poetic language as Silvius. From being the harsh mistress she becomes the desperate lover, and in her long speech at the end of the scene we have a delightful and rather moving picture of her confused emotions. She resolves to write a letter to the disguised Rosalind, who, when she receives it, is amazed by its shrill tone. Rosalind determines to put Phebe in her place, and it is just this hardness which Phebe finds so attractive. Eventually, Rosalind manipulates Phebe into promising that she will marry Silvius if – for any reason – she cannot marry

Ganymede. Of course, when Ganymede is finally shown to be Rosalind herself, Phebe is amazed and disappointed. However, she honours her promise to marry Silvius.

Thus, in the character of Phebe, Shakespeare amusingly presents the whole range of pastoral love: from adoration to cruelty; comic situations; and finally, as with all the lovers in the play, the development of love into a stable marriage.

CORIN

The old shepherd Corin is a crucial part of Shakespeare's pastoral world. Certainly, he amuses us with his simple rustic ways, just as he does Touchstone, who exercises his wit upon him in Act III, Scene ii. But Corin is not simply a figure of fun. He clearly loves the country life that he leads, and his simplistic directness and kindly honesty move us and show us something of the earthy wholesomeness of country life. We have said that Shakespeare was fully aware that life in the countryside was not just a simple idyll, and he uses the character of Corin to develop this. When we first meet Corin, we see something of the hardships of country life: a hard master, lack of money and insecurity.

We also see in Corin a natural and spontaneous generosity when he offers to provide Rosalind, Celia and Touchstone with food and shelter. Although Corin is too old, of course, to be a true pastoral lover, the scene in which he talks to Silvius again shows his kindly understanding. Thus, although Corin is only a minor character, he touches on the themes of *As You Like It* in many ways.

DUKE SENIOR

Shakespeare's presentation of Duke Senior – although he is given no real name – is rich and complex. We must read and study his words with the greatest care if we are ever to appreciate the true subtlety of the way in which Shakespeare presents the pastoral life.

We first hear of the banished Duke when the wrestler Charles derides his life in the Forest of Arden, where, we are told, the Duke and his friends 'fleet the time carelessly as they did in the golden world'. Here is the idyll of life in the country, a life without worry or responsibility, discomfort or problems. It is a dream and an illusion. But, in the context of the savage and unstable world of the usurper Duke Frederick, it appears particularly attractive. All those who are driven from the world of the court find themselves drawn inevitably to the Forest of Arden, where Duke Senior has managed to convince himself that he is entirely happy. But we should bear in mind that when, at the end of the play, he has been given his dukedom back, he leaves the Forest of Arden with barely a second thought. It is the world of the court in which he truly belongs, and his stay in the Forest of Arden is merely an interlude which he tries to make as delightful as possible. The happiness of the pastoral world, Shakespeare will show us, is in some senses an illusion. (For a discussion of the various ways in which Shakespeare presents illusion and then unmasks it in *As You Like It*, see pp. 84–5.)

We first meet Duke Senior at the beginning of Act II. If we read his first speech very attentively, then we shall see that while the Forest of Arden does indeed have its delights, they are nonetheless impaired by harsher facts. The courtiers do feel 'the penalty of Adam', the wind is cold, there is death here. Although a modern audience tends to be more sensitive about such things than Shakespeare's would have been, there is genuine pathos in the First Lord's description of the death of a stag. Whether they recognize it or not, Duke Senior and the others have brought death into the forest.

But Duke Senior is no fool. He has an intelligent man's sense of humour, which allows him both to be amused by and to see through Jaques's affectations. It is he who exposes the satirist as a sometime 'libertine'. Another aspect of his goodness is that the Duke is also a gentleman: he is courteous and able to appreciate the sufferings of others. This, combined with his natural authority, is made clear to us when Orlando bursts in on the feast (Act II, Scene vii). His charity towards old Adam reminds us of the virtuous world that existed before the Duke was ousted by his usurper brother.

It is part of the artificial nature of the pastoral convention (see pp. 33, 84–7) that the Duke does not recognize his daughter Rosalind through her disguise, but it is also important to notice that it is to him, as the seat of real authority, that all the characters turn at the end of the play to have their marriages approved. Duke Senior tries to bid Jaques join in this happy reunion, but in this he fails. Duke Senior, as is proper, provides generous entertainment at the end, but we should notice that, for all his praise of the pastoral life, he is keen enough to take back his throne at the end of the play.

DUKE FREDERICK

Duke Frederick is in many ways similar to Oliver. He is a 'stage villain' out of melodrama. His sudden changes of mood – for example, when he exiles Rosalind, calls his own daughter a fool, and seizes Oliver's possessions – allow us to see the sort of violent and unstable man who would indeed usurp the throne of a kingdom. At the start of the play Duke Frederick personifies hatred, violence and destruction.

Again, like Oliver, he goes through a sudden and complete conversion. When he is told of the many young men who rush to join Duke Senior in the Forest of Arden, he vows to seek them out and destroy them. On his way he is converted to a holy life by an old hermit. Nothing could be more unlikely or, in some ways, more ridiculous. But we have learned to accept this sort of thing as a typical and amusing aspect of the pastoral convention. Duke Frederick vows to live henceforth as a hermit, a man of holy works. What is perhaps most interesting about this is that 'the melancholy Jaques' sees that he must join him rather than the reconciled lovers at the end of the play.

ADAM

Adam appears only in the first half of the play. He represents many of the qualities that have recently been destroyed in the dukedom: loyalty, honesty, decency, friendship. In many respects, he serves as a foil to the more important characters. Oliver's appalling treatment of him arouses our sympathy and underlines Oliver's heartlessness before his conversion. More importantly, Adam's complete devotion to Orlando shows us both what true friendship and loyal service are, and also reveals that Orlando has the depth and sympathy to appreciate these qualities. Shakespeare is subtle in the presentation of Adam. If we are not careful, we will see him in too sentimental a way and consider him an impossibly good old man. But notice that this is not all that Shakespeare has to show us. First, although we are indeed moved by Adam's loyalty and his vision of his declining years – what he describes as 'unregarded age in corners thrown' – we also smile at the old man's garrulous ways. Orlando has some difficulty in understanding what he has to say when he is describing Oliver's plots against him after the wrestling match. But Adam has one final and very important contribution to make to the play, and he makes it in silence. We have learned to love and respect Adam for the virtues he shows. When Orlando carries him in to Duke Senior's feast, this very touching image of a strong and kindly youth charitably caring for a very weak old man serves to make a mockery of the harsh and cynical view of life that Jaques has put forward in his famous 'Seven Ages of Man' speech.

LE BEAU

Le Beau is a fop, a character Shakespeare was particularly keen on showing in his plays. He is affected, ridiculous apparently heartless, and a parasite in Duke Frederick's realm. A good actor will make us laugh at him not only through his words – notice how Rosalind and Celia run circles round him – but also through his ridiculous poses and mannerisms. Touchstone reproves him for his heartlessness in relishing the story of the old man whose three sons were broken at the wrestling match. But there are few simple characters in *As You Like It*. On the last occasion that we meet Le Beau, he warns Orlando of Duke Frederick's violent temperament and hopes to meet Orlando again 'in a better world than this'.

CHARLES

Charles is above all a 'muscle man'. He is very proud of his strength and wrestles for his honour, but is defeated by Orlando. He has some vestiges of human feeling – for example, when he tries to have Oliver dissuade his brother from entering the contest. However, Charles is a simple man and is easily convinced by Oliver that Orlando is a villain. Thus convinced, he relishes the idea of destroying Orlando, but in fact it is he who is vanquished.

SIR OLIVER MARTEXT

Sir Oliver Martext is, as his name implies, a foolish and illiterate priest. He is the man that Touchstone has arranged should marry him to Audrey, but when Jaques convinces Touchstone that he should not be 'married under a bush like a beggar', he is dismissed. Sir Oliver was entitled to a fee for conducting the marriage and leaves vowing that he shall have it. However, we do not see him again.

HYMEN: THE GOD OF MARRIAGE

Just as the song which the pages sing to Touchstone and Audrey gives to the play a special magic and poetry, so the appearance of 'a masquer representing Hymen' provides the closing moments of the play with a sense of beauty, mystery and harmony. In *As You Like It* love ends happily in marriage, and the appearance of Hymen, exquisitely dressed and accompanied by music, is a wonderful device for suggesting these qualities. His appearance is both the most artificial moment in the play and also one of the most beautiful. Through his music, his song and his words, we are prepared for the final resolution of the plot.

Themes

LOVE AND THE PASTORAL WORLD

On p. 33 we discussed the pastoral convention and noted that it was a particular type of literature with its own rules. We saw that pastoral concerns itself with dramatic adventures lived out by disguised aristocrats in a never-never world of shepherds. We also saw that one of the particular concerns of the pastoral convention is love, and in *As You Like It* Shakespeare both shows us a wide variety of love-affairs and gently points out their 'ridiculous' side.

The country life of pastoral is meant to be in direct contrast to the life of the court. This is very clear in *As You Like It*. The court is a place of violence, cruelty, arbitrary power and unhappiness. The Forest of Arden, on the other hand, is a place of innocence and delight. But we should be careful. The contrast is not a simple one. Shakespeare knew perfectly well that the real countryside is not a place that is simply idyllic, and although his Forest of Arden and those who live in it certainly have their delightfully innocent side, there is more to Shakespeare's presentation of country life than simple escapism. Duke Senior, when we are first introduced to him in Act II, Scene i, may praise the joys of the pastoral world, but, as we have seen, his speeches are full of ambiguity: things are not quite what they seem. The wind does blow and it is cold. The hunters do bring death and suffering to the forest. When Rosalind, Celia and Touchstone first arrive in the Forest of Arden, they are almost in tears with exhaustion and wish that they were back at the court. Throughout *As You Like It* we must be aware that all is not always as it seems to be. This is particularly obvious when we come to the presentation of love.

Throughout much of the play Rosalind is in her disguise as Ganymede, and when she first meets Orlando so dressed, in the Forest of Arden, the situation is meant to be ridiculous and we laugh at its absurdities. Here is a beautiful young woman whom cruel circumstances have obliged to disguise herself as a man. Orlando, also a fugitive from injustice, is passionately in love with Rosalind, but agrees to submit to a 'cure' from what he thinks is a young boy trained by a wise uncle. Such artificiality as this is a standard part of the pastoral convention.

But Shakespeare is doing far more than simply making us laugh. Through disguise, through appearance rather than reality, the lovers' feelings are being tested out. Rosalind, as we know, is head over heels in love, and her speeches both to Celia and to Orlando in Act III are wonderfully varied, ranging from intense excitement to the melancholy which affects all true lovers. We see also the healthy earthiness of her passion, her resilient wit, her love of life and the genuine pain into which she is thrown when it appears that Orlando is unfaithful and fails to turn up to their meeting. Such a range of emotions is both complex and very engaging. We are swept up into the energy of Rosalind's feelings. But we should also notice that though these feelings are very strong, the real Rosalind, beneath her disguise, has her feet very firmly on the ground. She can love quite as intensely as anyone else in the play, but she is quick to see through pretension and the poetic fantasies with which Orlando embellishes his love in the way that Silvius does. For example, when Orlando declares that he will die if he is rejected by Rosalind (disguised as Ganymede), she says (IV, i, 85–8):

> The poor world is almost six thousand years old, and in all this time there was not any man died in his own person, videlicet, in a love-cause.

Orlando, now that he is in the Forest of Arden, is happy to play the part of the ridiculous lover. He goes through all the proper motions: sighing, wandering about, writing rather bad love-poems. There is a degree of sheer affectation in this. He is playing a role. He may have convinced himself, but Rosalind, with her deeper intuition, is aware of something of the falseness in this. It is just this intuition and intelligence of Rosalind's that allows her to test Orlando's feelings. She manages to prove to Orlando that love is a species of madness and she offers to cure him in a most bizarre way. Orlando must pretend that Rosalind disguised as Ganymede is really Rosalind herself.

Orlando will find that Ganymede proves to be so contrary, so difficult a lover that he will eventually abandon love altogether. It is interesting that Orlando agrees to undertake the cure; but you should notice that Rosalind plays her part so skilfully that what she really does is fascinate Orlando completely and take over the wooing herself. It is Rosalind, the beautiful girl disguised as a boy, who really takes the initiative in love. Orlando, the man, whom we might expect to do the wooing, is really the one who is being led.

But Orlando's true feelings run deeper than the affectation he shows in the third and fourth acts of the play. His real need for Rosalind emerges when his reformed brother tells him that he has fallen in love with Celia and promised to marry her. Orlando is made suddenly aware of his great loneliness without Rosalind (V, ii, 41–5):

> But, O, how bitter a thing it is to look into happiness through another man's eyes! By so much the more shall I tomorrow be at the height of heart-heaviness, by how much I shall think my brother happy in having what he wishes for.

Rosalind overhears this sincere outpouring by Orlando and is moved by it, and just as she took the initiative in the courting, so now she must take the initiative in bringing events to the point where she may reveal her real identity and so prepare for her marriage to Orlando.

Marriage is the true end of love in *As You Like It*. Just as Rosalind solves Orlando's problems by dispelling the illusion she has created – by stepping out of her disguise and revealing her true identity – so she prepares the way for Silvius's marriage to the woman he loves. Orlando shows many of the excesses of the conventional lover, but Silvius shows even more. It is he who declares that true lovers run through 'many actions most ridiculous'. Nonetheless, beneath all this, Silvius's feelings are deep and true. Phebe, on the other hand, who has been indulging excessively in the role of the cruel mistress, has to have her illusions torn away before she can settle down to true, married happiness. She has to be humiliated by her impossible love for Ganymede and, when she has learnt her lesson, take up her role as Silvius's wife. The third couple in the play – Oliver and Celia – also discover that marriage is the true end of love. We do not see the development of their affair; we are only told about it. Oliver, however, like the other lovers in the play, has to go through a transformation before he is worthy. The evil brother of the opening scenes has to be shown the error of his ways and undergo a complete conversion before he can find his happiness. Finally, we should look at the relationship between Touchstone and Audrey. This, as we have seen, is a relationship more obviously based on physical desire than the others in the play. Although it too ends in marriage, Jaques makes perfectly clear that the happiness of this marriage will not last for very long. Touchstone and Audrey have married in haste, and we suspect that they will later repent at their leisure. This stops the beautifully harmonious ending of the play from appearing either too perfect or too sentimental.

There is another type of love discussed in *As You Like It*: it is a sense of goodness and charity towards all people – the opposite of the hatred and violence of life in court. We should notice that just as the young lovers discover their feelings and resolve their problems in the Forest of Arden, so the two villains of the play – Oliver and Duke Frederick – learn this sort of love in the Forest of Arden as well. Oliver's conversion to decent human feelings takes place after he has been rescued by his brother. Duke Frederick, who, we are told, has ridden out of the court to bring death and destruction to those in the Forest, is similarly converted when he arrives there. Through one of those highly unlikely but attractive reversals of fortune that characterize both *As You Like It* and the pastoral convention, Duke Frederick meets a hermit and undergoes a sudden and total conversion to a good life.

The Forest of Arden thus lies at the centre of Shakespeare's play and at the heart of the pastoral convention. It is a place of ambiguity. Things are not always what they seem to be. It is a place of gaiety, charm and innocence, but also a place of cruelty and suffering. Above all, it is a place of growth and change, a place where people discover what is true. Finally, when all the problems have been resolved, it is a place that nearly everyone leaves to go back to the real world of the reformed court. Only Jaques and Duke Frederick, men who have no real place in the happy, harmonious world of the reformed court, are left behind to lead more melancholy lives.

SATIRE AND MELANCHOLY

As You Like It, as we have seen, is a play that delights in artificiality
and absurdity. This is part of its attractiveness. One of the ways in
which Shakespeare highlights these aspects of his play is through
presenting their opposites: melancholy, bitterness and cynicism. Much
of this is conveyed through the character of Jaques. In a play about love
and growing feeling, Jaques, as the 'Seven Ages of Man' speech shows,
has a vision of life as something bitter and ridiculous. Everything that
he sees – and you should notice how Jaques glides through the play
watching, commentating but taking little part in the action – is a
suitable subject for satire. The hunting of stags, for instance, he
moralizes into a picture of man's foolishness and ingratitude. The song
that Amiens sings to the courtiers is bitterly parodied by Jaques to
make them look ridiculous. He tries to show up the absurdity of
Touchstone, Rosalind and Orlando, and we are well aware that many
of the comments that he makes are true. Nowhere is this more so than
in his parting comments on Touchstone's marriage.

But it is most important that we realize that Jaques represents only
one mood in the play, a mood that prevents *As You Like It* from
becoming sentimental but is not an end in itself. Jaques can see the
ridiculous side of everybody. He is unaware that everybody sees the
ridiculous side of him. The courtiers laugh at him, Duke Senior is
amused by him, Orlando is prepared to have a conversation with him
that is based on light-hearted, mutual contempt. Rosalind is so full of
life, energy and intelligence that she is quite impervious to Jaques's
criticisms and sees him for what he is: a rather affected and in some
ways rather ridiculous figure. Nonetheless, Jaques does make a very
powerful, imaginative impact on the play. Like all the characters whom
we really relish – Rosalind and Touchstone in particular – Jaques has
a marvellous facility with words. He can play with them, twist them
about, entertain us with them and, in his great 'Seven Ages of Man'
speech, really move and convince us. This speech, as we have said, is
a most powerful picture of human life as a cruel and ridiculous folly.
It is vivid, bitter, elegant and energetic. It is also untrue. For all its
power to convince us, for all Jaques's ability to show up the cruel and
absurd aspects of human life, there is far more to it than this speech
allows for. Convinced as we momentarily are by what he says, when

Orlando enters carrying the exhausted Adam, and the Duke, with simple and unaffected human kindness, gives them food and protection, then Jaques's bitterness evaporates. He has nothing further to say during the whole scene.

But Jaques is not the only source of satire in *As You Like It*. We have seen that Shakespeare himself gently satirizes the pastoral convention. He exaggerates the villainy of Oliver and Duke Frederick, so that while we are aware of how truly wicked they are, we nonetheless smile at them. Again, their conversions near the end of the play are so sudden, so complete and so unlikely that again we are tempted to smile. We have also mentioned that the widely popular pastoral convention was a form of escapist literature. It takes us into a deliberately artificial and highly contrived world, just as romantic fiction or spy stories do. Shakespeare, while thoroughly delighting in conventions, also shows their mildly ridiculous side. Duke Senior, for example, appears to thoroughly enjoy what he sees as the delightful, innocent world of the Forest of Arden. It is almost as if the Duke himself has read too many pastoral novels and can only see the Forest of Arden as an ideal place set in never-never land. Yet his speech in Act II, Scene i, shows that the Forest of Arden is not a simple, idyllic place. It is cold and death lurks in it. Again, the shepherds and rustics in the play are either, like William and Audrey, so simple as to be humorous parodies of what country people are conventionally thought to be like, or, like Silvius, so absurdly artificial that we can only be delighted that such highly improbable people can live in such a real forest. Finally, we should realize that Rosalind herself has a very sharp eye for absurd and pretentious behaviour. She exposes Phebe's affectation with some forcefulness, and she also creates the situation in which Orlando can make himself look ridiculous.

Thus, through a wide and subtle variety of means, Shakespeare satirizes the pastoral world while, at the same time, showing us the very real delights and human feelings that can exist in this world of the imagination.

Examination Questions

1. 'Love is merely a madness.'
   'Whoever loved that loved not at first sight?'

   What view of love does the play seem to take?

2. Read the following passage carefully and then answer the questions printed after it.

DUKE FREDERICK: Bear him away. What is thy name,
    young man?
ORLANDO: Orlando, my liege; the youngest son of
    Sir Rowland de Boys.
DUKE FREDERICK: I would thou hadst been son to some man
    else.
    The world esteem'd thy father honourable,
    But I did find him still mine enemy.
    Thou shouldst have better pleas'd me with this deed,   5
    Hadst thou descended from another house.
    But fare thee well; thou art a gallant youth;
    I would thou hadst told me of another father.
        [*Exeunt Duke, Train, and Le Beau.*]
CELIA: Were I my father, coz, would I do this?   10
ORLANDO: I am more proud to be Sir Rowland's son,
    His youngest son – and would not change that calling
    To be adopted heir to Frederick.
ROSALIND: My father lov'd Sir Rowland as his soul,
    And all the world was of my father's mind;   15
    Had I before known this young man his son,
    I should have given him tears unto entreaties
    Ere he should thus have ventur'd.

CELIA: Gentle cousin,
  Let us go thank him, and encourage him;
  My father's rough and envious disposition   20
  Sticks me at heart. Sir, you have well deserv'd;
  If you do keep your promises in love
  But justly as you have exceeded all promise,
  Your mistress shall be happy.
ROSALIND: Gentleman,
      [*giving him a chain from her neck*]
  Wear this for me; one out of suits with fortune,   25
  That could give more, but that her hand lacks means.
  Shall we go, coz?
CELIA: Ay. Fare you well, fair gentleman.
ORLANDO: Can I not say 'I thank you'? My better parts
  Are all thrown down; and that which here stands up
  Is but a quintain, a mere lifeless block.   30
ROSALIND: He calls us back. My pride fell with my fortunes;
  I'll ask him what he would. Did you call, sir?
  Sir, you have wrestled well, and overthrown
  More than your enemies.
CELIA: Will you go, coz?
ROSALIND: Have with you. Fare you well.   35
      [*Exeunt Rosalind and Celia.*]
ORLANDO: What passion hangs these weights upon my tongue?
  I cannot speak to her, yet she urg'd conference.
  O poor Orlando, thou art overthrown!
  Or Charles or something weaker masters thee.

(i) What has the Duke just seen to make him say: *Bear him away.
What is thy name, young man* (line 1)?   [2]

(ii) What is the meaning of: *still* (line 5), *coz* (line 10), *ere* (line 18),
sticks me at heart (line 21)?   [5]

(iii) Put into clear modern English lines 21–6 (*Sir, you have well
deserved ... but that her hand lacks means*).   [8]

(iv) What does this extract tell us of the characters of
  (*a*) Duke Frederick,   [4]
  (*b*) Celia,   [4]

(*c*) Rosalind,   [6]

(*d*) Orlando?   [6]

(v) In this extract there are several references to wrestling. How does Shakespeare use them to convey Rosalind's and Orlando's reactions to each other?   [5]

(*Oxford and Cambridge Schools Examination Board, 1983*)

3. Read the following passage carefully and answer the questions beneath it.

JAQUES: I prithee, pretty youth, let me be better acquainted with thee.

ROSALIND: They say you are a melancholy fellow.

JAQUES: I am so; I do love it better than laughing.

ROSALIND: Those that are in extremity of either are abomin-   5
able fellows, and betray themselves to every modern censure
worse than drunkards.

JAQUES: Why, 'tis good to be sad and say nothing.

ROSALIND: Why then, 'tis good to be a post.

JAQUES: I have neither the scholar's melancholy, which is   10
emulation; nor the musician's, which is fantastical; nor the
courtier's, which is proud; nor the soldier's, which is
ambitious; nor the lawyer's, which is politic; nor the lady's,
which is nice; nor the lover's, which is all these; but it is a
melancholy of mine own, compounded of many simples, ex-   15
tracted from many objects, and, indeed, the sundry con-
templation of my travels; in which my often rumination wraps
me in a most humorous sadness.

ROSALIND: A traveller! By my faith, you have great reason to
be sad. I fear you have sold your own lands to see other men's;   20
then to have seen much and to have nothing is to have rich
eyes and poor hands.

JAQUES: Yes, I have gain'd my experience.

[*Enter Orlando.*]

ROSALIND: And your experience makes you sad. I had rather
have a fool to make me merry than experience to make me sad   25
and to travel for it too.

ORLANDO: Good day, and happiness, dear Rosalind!

JAQUES: Nay, then, God buy you, an you talk in blank
verse.

ROSALIND: Farewell, Monsieur Traveller; look you lisp and   30
wear strange suits, disable all the benefits of your own country,
be out of love with your nativity, and almost chide God for
making you that countenance you are; or I will scarce think
you have swam in a gondola. [*Exit Jaques*] Why, how now,
Orlando! where have you been all this while? You a lover! An   35
you serve me such another trick, never come in my sight more.

ORLANDO: My fair Rosalind, I come within an hour of my
promise.

ROSALIND: Break an hour's promise in love! He that will divide
a minute into a thousand parts, and break but a part of the   40
thousand part of a minute in the affairs of love, it may be said
of him that Cupid hath clapp'd him o' th' shoulder, but I'll
warrant him heart-whole.

ORLANDO: Pardon me, dear Rosalind.   45

ROSALIND: Nay, an you be so tardy, come no more in my sight.
I had as lief be woo'd of a snail.

ORLANDO: Of a snail!

(i) Explain briefly why Rosalind and Orlando are meeting in the
forest. [6]

(ii) Give the meaning of the words: *emulation* (line 11); *politic* (line
13); *nice* (line 14); *simples* (line 15). [4]

(iii) Summarize Rosalind's words to Jaques (lines 30–34 *Farewell
... gondola*) (you need not give a word for word translation) and say
what these lines show about Rosalind's attitude towards Jaques. [10]

(iv) Comment on the relationship between Rosalind and Orlando as
shown in this passage. [6]

(v) Compare Jaques's humour and Rosalind's wit as shown in this
passage. [6]

(vi) What does Jaques decide to do at the end of the play, and how
far is this decision in keeping with what we learn of his character in the
above passage? [8]

(*Oxford and Cambridge Schools Examination Board, 1979*)

4. All the world's a stage
   And all the men and women merely players:
   They have their exits and their entrances,
   And one man in his time plays many parts,
   His acts being seven ages. At first the infant,
   Mewling and puking in the nurse's arms;
   And then the whining schoolboy, with his satchel,
   And shining morning face, creeping like snail
   Unwillingly to school. And then the lover,
   Sighing like furnace, with a woeful ballad
   Made to his mistress' eyebrow. Then a soldier,
   Full of strange oaths, and bearded like the pard,
   Jealous in honour, sudden and quick in quarrel,
   Seeking the bubble reputation
   Even in the cannon's mouth. And then the justice,
   In fair round belly with good capon lin'd,
   With eyes severe, and beard of formal cut,
   Full of wise saws and modern instances;
   And so he plays his part. The sixth age shifts
   Into the lean and slipper'd pantaloon,
   With spectacles on nose, and pouch on side,
   His youthful hose well sav'd, a world too wide
   For his shrunk shank; and his big manly voice,
   Turning again toward childish treble, pipes
   And whistles in his sound. Last scene of all,
   That ends this strange eventful history,
   Is second childishness, and mere oblivion,
   Sans teeth, sans eyes, sans taste, sans everything.

(*Associated Examining Board, 1980*)

Choose four of the seven ages of man and show how Shakespeare's description is accurate and illuminating.

MORE ABOUT PENGUINS, PELICANS
AND PUFFINS

For further information about books available from Penguins please write to Dept EP, Penguin Books Ltd, Harmondsworth, Middlesex UB7 0DA.

In the U.S.A.: For a complete list of books available from Penguins in the United States write to Dept DG, Penguin Books, 299 Murray Hill Parkway, East Rutherford, New Jersey 07073.

In Canada: For a complete list of books available from Penguins in Canada write to Penguin Books Canada Ltd, 2801 John Street, Markham, Ontario L3R 1B4.

In Australia: For a complete list of books available from Penguins in Australia write to the Marketing Department, Penguin Books Australia Ltd, P.O. Box 257, Ringwood, Victoria 3134.

In New Zealand: For a complete list of books available from Penguins in New Zealand write to the Marketing Department, Penguin Books (N.Z.) Ltd, Private Bag, Takapuna, Auckland 9.

In India: For a complete list of books available from Penguins in India write to Penguin Overseas Ltd, 706 Eros Apartments, 56 Nehru Place, New Delhi 110019.